Collaborative Healing

A "Shorter" Therapy Approach for Survivors of Sexual Abuse

MARK HIRSCHFELD, LCSW-C, BCD
AND
JILL B. CODY, M.A.

ISBN: 0-9749711-1-1

**For information on this and other PESI HealthCare manuals
and audiocassettes, please call**

800-843-7763

Acknowledgments

Mark Hirschfeld

To my wonderful families, the one who created me and the one that sustains me. I am very lucky. To my parents Karl and Rose who gave me the philosophy of life, values, and desire to help those who were in need of a "supportive ear" regardless of their struggles and to give to others in a way that makes a difference.

To my wife and best friend, Robin, and Taryn, Karlin and Jordy, without whose love and support none of this would have been possible.

I am truly grateful to those have helped and inspired me in the writing of this manuscript. These include all those friends and family who proofread the drafts and politely kept asking "How's the book going?" Now I can finally say "Done" Thanks for all your understanding and support. A special thank you goes to my co-author Jill Cody who had the patience and wisdom to re-focus my energy toward completion of the manuscript. Her positive "spin" on the trials and tribulations of becoming "published" were invaluable.

I want to thank the colleagues who have shared information, cases and time with me as I begin the process of formulating the message of the manuscript. I am also grateful to the organizations and groups who have sponsored my workshops and the people who have attended them. I have learned a great deal from you.

These acknowledgments would not be complete without mention of my clients, who have trusted me enough to share their lives with me and, in doing so, have taught me a great lesson about how people change and move forward despite the traumas of their lives. Thank you so very much.

The case examples presented in the book are based on real people and their experiences, but I have changed names and other details to protect the anonymity of the people and their families.

Jill Cody

I want to acknowledge the continual and outstanding support of my wonderful husband, Richard, who has been the wind underneath my wings for all of my adult life. I cannot underscore enough the contributions of my mother and father, Irene and Herbert Bluethenthal who gave me unconditional love and security growing up that allowed me to have the internal resources, empathy and values necessary to help others who have not been so fortunate. My brother-in-law, Jerry Friedlander, contributed his legal expertise in negotiating me through the maze of the publishing world's contracts and intricacies.

I especially appreciate and acknowledge the contributions of Ron Klein, my mentor, my colleague and my friend for his gift of making Ericksonian Hypnosis and NLP interventions come alive for me, for his magnificent model for training and presenting, and for his personal encouragement to follow my dream.

I thank Mark Hirschfeld for inviting me to participate in bringing this book to reality. It has been a fun and enlightening experience to work with him to put clinical principles and events into written form. It is my hope that others can build on the ideas and techniques we have presented, and can further disseminate these healing methods.

About the Authors

Mark Hirschfeld LCSW-C, BCD, is a board certified diplomate in clinical social work. For the last 20 years he has specialized in the assesment and treatment of incestuous families, including survivors and offenders. He served as the director for a treatment program for families involved with incest at a large mental health clinic in suburban Washington, D.C. He maintains an active private and consultative practice. Mark has presented professional workshops, seminars, in-service training and consultation throughout the United States.

Jill Cody, a nationally Certified Clinical Mental Health Counselor and a Licensed Clinical Professional Counselor in Maryland, earned her Masters Degree in Counseling Psychology from Hood College. In addition, Jill received Post-Graduate training in Clinical Hypnosis at the American Hypnosis Training Academy in Silver Spring, and is currently a trainer for that organization. She travels extensively teaching clinical hypnosis skills to other Mental Health professionals, as well as maintaining a private psychotherapy practice in Frederick, Maryland.

For several years, Jill served as the Stress Management Instructor for the Wellness Center at Frederick Memorial Hospital.

An active member of the Frederick Toastmaster Club and the National Speakers Association for many years, she is an enthusiastic public speaker.

Jill is married, and in her spare time has managed to raise 3 sons to adulthood. A charter member of the Rotary Club of Carroll Creek in Frederick, Jill is a past president. She is currently serving as the president of the Licensed Clinical Professional Counselors of Maryland.

Table of Contents

Introduction

This book is born from the recent influx of clients who have either initiated therapy because of their experiences of incest or sexual abuse in their past, or who have come to recognize the impact of these experiences on the presenting problems and/or relationship issues they face in their lives. When they finally put the pieces together, it is as if a light bulb turns on in their mind, and suddenly the negative feelings of guilt, inner pain, and disgust begin to make sense. They can now begin the healing process. Using the concept of a collaborative treatment plan based on our training and skills as well as on the client's unique history and personal resources, we want to present strategies and specific techniques that we have found helpful in treating this population.

Facilitating this healing can be equally stressful to the clinician taking on this responsibility as it is to the survivors of the abuse coping with the memories and the aftermath. We therapists are all empathic and caring people. (If we were not, we would not have chosen counseling as our field of endeavor.) When we are told the stories of these atrocities, we are prone to experiencing a secondary trauma that can contribute to our own burnout or early retirement. We need multiple strategies not only to make our work with this population easier, but also to effectively nurture and take care of ourselves.

I (Mark) have been a psychotherapist for twenty-seven years and have worked with survivors of incest and sexual abuse during the last twenty. During this time, as I examined my own work, and spoke with other colleagues, I became aware that the issues raised in working with the survivors of sexual abuse are potentially some of the most difficult for any clinician to face. I have also come to realize and witness the reality that victims can and do heal. They recover from the symptoms of sexual abuse, and go on to lead positive, healthy lives. Our goal as clinicians is to establish a collaborative relationship with our clients to guide them in the discovery and acceptance of their internal resources as well as abilities to recover. This is a process by which we assist them in going "inside" and looking at themselves, as they begin to acknowledge and feel their own sense of positive worth and self-esteem. The recognition of these feelings with which they probably could not have identified prior to coming to therapy, become more apparent. Witnessing this change in many of the clients with whom I have worked has truly been one of the most rewarding experiences I have had as a therapist.

I (Jill) have been a practicing psychotherapist for the past 25 years. One of my specialties is to help clients recover from experiences of physical and sexual abuse, and other symptoms of post-traumatic stress. Many clients express concern about wanting to avoid a recurrence of the pain connected with remembering the abuse. They would just as soon put it in the past and leave it alone, even though they still suffer from the effects of this abuse on their life.

One metaphor which I like to use to describe the value of going through the intense experience of counseling is that of healing from a deep cut. If it is left alone, it will probably scab over and eventually heal, but the person who has that injury is prone to infections or scarring. Although it hurts to have that cut cleaned out, and have stitches put in, it will promote a more genuine healing which has the best chance of success. A powerful intervention, in and of itself, is to offer a validation of the client's account of that experience and provide the expectation and hope of healing from it, with assurances that the interventions used will protect them from re-experiencing pain. Even the fact that we can hear the story with all of that concomitant ugliness, and still accept the client as a worthwhile person is a strong signal to the client that the healing has begun. I have indeed found this work to be an intensely rewarding professional experience.

The purpose in writing this book is to impart certain ideas, mind-sets, and assumptions, as well as specific techniques which we have found can make this work more satisfying to both ourselves and our clients.

This book presents these as options, possibilities and recommendations, and thus helps the reader formulate for him or herself an understanding of how to approach this treatment population. "Sexual abuse," as we have used it throughout the book relates to the inappropriate overt or covert sexual behaviors involving siblings, parents, extended family and all others who have caretaker or custodial roles with a child. These roles are typically the most damaging because when sexuality is introduced, it provokes feelings of betrayal, loss of innocence and role confusion. We have included case examples from our professional experiences for clarity. Some of these observations may be validations of what you already may do; others may be new thoughts, perspectives, and suggestions to add to your professional "tool kit" of interventions.

Our first chapter, entitled "Why This? Why Now?" explores the issues of the impact of the work on the therapist, allowing us to evaluate how we respond to the issues brought up by this population. In our professional lingo, we call this personal intense reaction "countertransference." We have to be educated about this possibility as the best defense against allowing our empathy and caring to blind our objectivity and subsequent ability to be helpful. The section on "Therapist Self-Care," reflects on the need to take care of ourselves to prevent burnout or over-identification with the distress and untenable situations and stories that clients present. Specific suggestions for a shift of our perspectives and some strategies for implementing these new perspectives are discussed.

"Replaying the Tapes," is the second chapter and focuses on those belief systems which clients have adopted as defense mechanisms to survive, and which now negatively impact their lives. In order to help clients construct the appropriate tracks which will guide their personal trains away from disaster, we need an understanding of the complex and limiting belief systems which filter their experiences and responses. There are specific interventions which will help them construct more appropriate and empowering belief systems.

"The Power of the Therapeutic Alliance," our third chapter, contrasts Ericksonian approaches to counseling with the more traditional therapies. Over time and through experience, the approaches to the treatment of incest and sexual abuse have gone through a metamorphosis of sorts. The staunch and inflexible theoretical frameworks of traditional psychotherapy have become unwieldy and impractical as the means to meet the diverse needs of this population. When therapists can use solution-focused and Ericksonian methodologies, they allow themselves to be spontaneous and creative in the therapeutic process. Consequently the client will feel cared about and validated. This gives a more in-depth understanding of our mindset, assumptions and the rationale for our model of working with clients.

A practical model of collaboration, explored in the fourth chapter entitled "A Therapeutic Model" is a road map of mindsets, strategies and techniques in treating survivors of sexual abuse. In writing this together, we were amazed to discover how closely connected our unique styles of working were. Obviously a model is not a mandate. Our intention is to give you a starting point to explore, add your own personality, training and counseling experiences. This model will *not* work with every client. No model does. That being said, we have found that the concepts of identifying the unique needs of each individual, identifying and reframing the presented problems, and empowering each to use the internal resources they already possess or to help them create new ones helps the client feel in control in areas where control had not existed before.

The strategies related in Chapter Five on "Forging the Therapeutic Alliance" comprise the first stage of our model. The concerns of establishing rapport in preparation for doing therapeutic work with this population may be different from others with whom you are used to working. Certain issues of proximity, touch, tonality and language may be triggers of a previous abusive situation even though these may not be in the foreground of our clients' thoughts. In the words of greater minds than ours, *"It is better to be safe than sorry."* If we damage or lose rapport with our clients, even unintentionally, it is a long road back reestablishing trust and an environment conducive to healing.

In the sixth chapter, "Challenging the Limiting Belief Systems," we focus on the second phase of the therapeutic model. We present specific strategies for reformulating those limiting or negative belief systems which would ultimately interfere with whatever positive behavioral changes we may recommend in the best of our cognitive-behavioral traditions. We can offer more positive, empowering beliefs to replace them, and once they have been integrated inside, the client will be ready to accept different ways of thinking and behaving.

"Integrating the Functional Adult with the Healed Inner Child" which represents the third phase of the model is the subject of the Chapter Seven. Subsequent to reformulating and integrating the systems of negative beliefs successfully, it is our opportunity and responsibility to give the client an education about nurturing, comforting and healing the "inner child" who has been so betrayed and injured. It is also incumbent on us to help our clients to allow their appropriate adult coping skills that they have developed over the years to help provide the security that they will be protected from the perpetrators now that they are adults. Specific suggestions and examples are offered.

Chapter Eight explores both the pros and cons of confrontation and disclosure to the perpetrator(s) of the abuse or to other family members as well as how to handle the inevitability of "Termination of Therapy." The considerations, risks and possible consequences of confrontation need to be considered intently and discussed before the survivor of the abuse takes those risks. It is important to consider all the aspects of our client's personal ecology or circumstances which might be affected by these actions. These considerations and alternatives are explored from the point of view of continuing to provide protection for our clients. The inevitability of ending the therapy necessitates that we do early and adequate planning for this eventuality. It should not be our intention to foster client dependency on us. Empowering our clients to heal means that they appreciate and accept they will have the ability and appropriate strategies to take care of themselves. We can help them predict the stimuli or situations which might trigger negative responses, and inoculate them against relapsing into negative emotions or behaviors, in spite of any hardships that reality may generate. We need to give the therapeutic process meaning and relevance to their future to facilitate further acceptance and integration of their progress and successes.

There are other aspects of abuse which may be ignored or disregarded because one does not recognize the signs or symptoms of their existence. The need to "Shift Our Perspectives" about covert or hidden abuse and the whole issue of sibling abuse is the focus of Chapter Nine. The many myths and misunderstandings about sibling abuse pervade our culture at both ends of the spectrum from those who fear that any experimentation or play is abusive to those who ignore the most egregious examples as 'playing doctor.' Power struggles can generate these occurrences or result from them. When this dynamic can be understood, we can reduce the negative effects and by-products.

We end this exploration in the Tenth chapter by a brief examination of "Diagnostic Errors and Oversights" focusing on how we may neglect to ask about abuse experiences in our intake interviews or fail to follow through with appropriate questions when clients express hesitation, labile emotions or anger which seems out of proportion to what is being discussed. Even experienced therapists will often confuse symptoms of post-traumatic stress with evidence of Borderline Personality Disorder thus denying the clients an opportunity for more successful interventions that are relevant to treating Post Traumatic Stress resulting from the abuse. Conversely, we must protect ourselves from making assumptions that every problem generates from "repressed memories" of sexual abuse.

For the purposes of clarity in writing, we will use only one set of personal pronouns—"she" or "her," to represent a *client* unless otherwise specified. The pronouns "he" and "him" generally are used to indicate a therapist, unless otherwise specified or appropriate. You can be assured that the reference is to either sex, and is not meant to be construed as preferential. Names of therapists and clients alike have been invented to protect the privacy and anonymity of both.

We believe that people do heal; that they can become more aware of themselves with our therapeutic assistance, and develop a healthy and satisfactory outlook for their lives. Treatment must be flexible enough to allow them to achieve this new outlook in only the number of sessions that the particular client needs, so as not to prolong the process. This collaboration involves letting clients help determine their own course of therapy.

This approach becomes time-sensitive rather than time-limited. In this age of managed care systems with which many clinicians are now confronted, the issue of limited sessions and the shorter duration of therapy tend to wreak havoc with our clinical sensitivity and desire to help the client resolve *all* of their issues. Clients are now being told by insurance companies that regardless of the nature and progress of symptoms, only a finite number of sessions will be approved.

Imagine the anxiety that an incest or abuse survivor entering into therapy must feel with the added burden to "hurry the process along, so as to cover all of their material in the allotted time. The need to find appropriate, shorter term, but respectful interventions that also allow for sensitivity to the issues, becomes paramount when working with survivors of incest and sexual abuse.

In this book we are attempting to convey to you the assumptions and values that have been helpful in working with victims of abuse and incest as we observe our clients move toward resolution. It is based on years of clinical work with clients, and studies and data collected over the years that have been presented in many workshops. The important values we stress that underlie all of this work include hope and respectfulness; validation and acknowledgment of symptoms; awareness and appreciation of one's own internal resources. We are delighted to share the successful strategies

that have worked to encourage our clients to change the limitin₄
beliefs and resource-less responses to their abuse.

All of our work is predicated on the idea that clients have all the
inner resources to formulate for themselves impactful solutions to
their therapeutic issues, and then carry them out, with our professional assistance. It is not the "old style" therapeutic experience
where the therapist is the "expert," imparting to the client her own
interpretation of that abuse experience. Rather, it is based on a philosophy that the client brings her own wisdom and knowledge of
what she needs to heal to the therapy process. Initially, we find that
our client often has a muted or distorted understanding of what is
happening inside of herself. However, when combined with a newly
gleaned understanding and acceptance of his inner resources, we
can collaborate with our client in formulating an acceptable way to
carry out those solutions in practical ways. We formulate a mutually respectful alliance to facilitate the client's desired outcome effi-
ciently and effectively. During the years of work with abuse and
incest survivors, we have discovered that using a combination of
treatment modalities, blending closely related and intertwined principles and techniques of therapy, is most effective in serving this
client population. The therapy techniques can be creatively rein-
vented to maintain a series of personalized and sensitive responses
for each client. In this regard, combining concepts of Solution-
Focused Therapy and Ericksonian Hypnosis with principles of cognitive therapy has been the most effective treatment approach. This
approach allows one to experiment and "go with" the experiences
that a client brings into the therapy room each week. When you
allow yourself this flexibility, the most appropriate intervention can
be designed for that particular client. There is no expectation of how
it is "supposed" to be, according to specific theoretical formulations.
There is a fluidity that allows the client and therapist to move
together within the therapeutic process where they accumulate both
positive and negative experiences, feelings, and resources. The client
can offer insight, motivation, resources, and memories during the
session while the therapist offers the strategies and approaches that
allow us both to move together toward his desired outcome. Many of
our clients have been unable to acknowledge the "unconscious" part
of them that is frequently the source of much of their psychologically limiting symptoms. Their unconscious is the equivalent of an
internal "psychological" storage bin.

At some time in the future, when triggered by some external
stimuli, often outside their awareness, the bin tips over and some of

the stored material spills out. This material often produces the experience of symptoms, and activates the inappropriate fears and behaviors that frequently bring them into therapy in the first place.

With Ericksonian hypnosis, we can assist the client by tapping into these unconscious messages before they erupt, and do so in a safer, more secure environment. Solution-Focused Therapy is a way of constructing solutions interactively, and provides a format whereby the client and therapist co-create solutions as quickly as rapport allows.

As Bill O'Hanlon would say, "Possibilities" abound. (O'Hanlon, 1996) The ability to create and achieve the desired changes in their lives emerges. Often to their great surprise, these clients develop a conscious positive dialogue for themselves and an increasing awareness of their issues. Without this awareness and acknowledgment, clients often get stuck in what they perceive to be evidence of "victimhood." Rather than maintaining their existing focus on problems, this approach provides a new outlook on possible solutions, freeing them to focus on strategies to control and or eradicate their symptoms. They are empowered to reclaim healthy patterns of perceiving and behaving or create them for the future. Tapping into these positive internal resources and concepts that facilitate the client's healing is what the therapy must do in order to be successful.

[1]

Why This? Why Now?

Understanding the Issues of Countertransference

> When you choose to earn your living by helping people who are in emotional pain, you're also making a choice to carry them on your back for awhile. Your patients will imprint you, like goslings who latch on to the first creature they see when they stick their heads out of the eggshell. If you can't handle it . . . become an accountant.
>
> J. Kellerman

Stella, a therapist with five years of clinical experience working with child victims and adult survivors of abuse, is overly cautious when her children want to play outside. She refuses to allow them to play without constant vigilance over them. Norma tends to dream about some of her clients, and at times finds her dreams getting more vivid in their context regarding acts of violence and brutality. Steve always saw himself as someone who could "deal with the tough cases," now finds himself increasingly irritable and angry. His recent behavior with his wife and children creates concern for him as he seems to have no clear understanding of why he acts the way he does. Mary, whose work as a Child Protective Services worker often requires her to be "on-call" by telephone, notices that whenever her telephone rings, she "flinches" and has visceral reactions that she can't explain.

What similarities could all these clinicians share? They are all attempting to deal with the predictable aftereffects of working with clients who have been sexually abused. The profound psycho-

1

logical "fallout" from exposure to this type of work is regularly overlooked when discussing the therapeutic process for our clients. The clinical term that describes what these clinicians are experiencing is regularly used, but frequently under-reported or misunderstood, is ***countertransference***.

This chapter addresses these issues of countertransference and the potential negative impact they pose for all of us as we proceed to work with our clients. We also discuss the techniques and strategies to help us learn how to be more self-protective in avoiding what may be seen as a "secondary traumatization" for those working closely with survivors of sexual abuse.

In reviewing the literature concerning the treatment of survivors of incest and sexual abuse, we found that any discussion of the issues relating to negative countertransference was placed near the end of the book. To the contrary, when working with the sexual abuse population, we have found it is essential that an understanding of the very significant issue of counter transference needs to be forged early in the formulation of the therapist's framework for treatment.

> (The) therapist's adequate support (of their clients) must be reinforced by their knowledge and emotional experience. Theoretical understanding alone is still not enough. Therapists who have had the opportunity to experience and work through their own traumatic past will be able to accompany patients on the path to truth about themselves and not hinder them on the way. Such therapists will not confuse their patients, make them anxious, or educate, instruct, misuse, or seduce them, for they no longer have to fear the eruption in themselves of feelings that were stifled long ago, and they know from experience the healing power of these feelings. (Miller, 1984)

Professionals who work with trauma survivors may experience profound psychological effects; effects that can remain with them for months or even years. To effectively come to grips with the intense personal issues involved in dealing with this population, we must understand the unique characteristics of this work, and its residual impact on our personae.

When we hear the horrors of survivors' stories, unresolved issues or fears are often stimulated in our own conscious or unconscious awareness. As a result, we tend to hide behind our own well-developed defense mechanisms. As responsible, ethical therapists, our initial mandate is to individually determine the vulnerabilities and strengths we contribute to the therapy process and those that we take from the therapy room each day. Two very important questions may give you the first clue to the psychological effects that doing trauma work can have on you.

1. Why do you work with this particular patient population?
2. What about this work interests, excites, and challenges you?

While there are no right or wrong answers, these are the *right questions* to ask yourself. It is important to spend some time considering your responses as these questions will serve to define your values and preferences more clearly. When you give clarity and concreteness to these ideas, you will build competence and confidence in your ability to truly help these individuals. If we ignore these questions, we are doing a disservice to both our clients and ourselves. We may allow biases or underlying assumptions and misinformation to affect how we approach clients in the therapy session. Therefore, there may be global implications regarding how both patient and clinician view the therapeutic relationship. To appropriately cope with the intense personal issues that are uncovered in working with these clients, we must understand the unique characteristics of this work, and its residual impact on us. Working with survivors of sexual abuse needs to be a result of choice. It is a commitment to see them through all the rough spots all the way to the healing.

Experience has taught us that it is difficult to simply treat this client population at our office for their 50-minute hour, and then wait another week to reengage. Because of the enormous amount of internal energy that is utilized, we inevitably tend to take these patients "home" with us. We think about treatment plans, or how we can intervene to create positive change. They are in the car with us, at social events with us, and sometimes they even invade or "share" our dreams, and our nightmares. There are times these patients have an impact on us, even when treatment has concluded?

Each of us may have entered this field for different reasons, and we have as many responses to the above questions as we have motivations. However, we probably share one basic common value: we want to be of service to clients, and to assist in facilitating their recovery.

Our responsibility is to create a safe and comfortable environment for all of our clients to tell their story. Whether or not they come in with a presenting issue of sexual abuse, they have important stories to tell about their lives. We have all been taught that active listening is an important skill, offering clients an unspoken, intuitive sense of safety and acceptance. This implicitly allows them to put their proverbial toes into the uncharted waters of therapy. We gather that information, and plan our interventions based on it. The one variable is our reaction to what we have heard—and how we feel about the processing of those particular sexual abuse issues. These various emotional responses or reactions are often referred to as "countertransference."

If we are uncomfortable with the thought of hearing these stories, we may deny their possibility by not asking the hard questions necessary to bring these issues up to the level to effectively deal with them in therapy. Perhaps we do not use body words relating to male or female anatomy such as "penis, vagina, breast, etc." It may be necessary to familiarize ourselves with the slang connected to these words. We may distance ourselves from the importance of this issue in our client's life, such as: *"Well, it probably wasn't a big deal back then; otherwise you would have dealt with it before now."* Another form of discomfort may even involve subtly placing blame on the client herself. *"You were really young then, and may have enjoyed the special attention your father gave you."* Some of us may identify with the victim and may feel empathy, in the form of "guilt" (particularly if the therapist is the same sex as the abuser), or an intense horror that this abuse would happen to a nice person. *"This should never happen to anybody like you."* On the other hand, some therapists may vicariously enjoy the "privileged voyeurism" of hearing the profane details of those scandalous stories.

Another form of this countertransference is even more insidious. It is when the therapist identifies with the client to the extent that he blurs the appropriate therapeutic boundaries. Some therapists have even had similar experiences in their own background.

Some self-assessment questions to ask yourself are: How personally involved do you get with your clients? Do you give them your home phone number? Do you run over the allotted time in your sessions? Does it take you longer to decompress after your session with these clients? You are not the parent, and cannot make up for the losses. The losses must be acknowledged and grieved for healing to occur.

The statistics are pretty clear. The vast majority of the people who acknowledge having been abused are women. In our experience, the ratio is about eight women for every one man. The gender of the therapist is significant to these survivors. I (Mark) raise this issue with my clients immediately. I approach it from the point of view that while I am an empathic clinician, I also understand that there may be some feeling about me being the same sex as the perpetrator, in a position to possibly take advantage of the client again. I want to let my clients know that if we decide to work together, it will be a collaborative decision. The hope is that perhaps this would be the first non-sexual, appropriate experience with a member of the opposite sex.

Even the most experienced therapists cannot be totally immune to the effects of helping clients work through intense posttraumatic responses. They must expect to be affected as a price of doing this work. They can, however, take steps to provide some degree of protection and relief for themselves from the most insidiously destructive effects. (Courtois, 1993)

According to Courtois, countertransference refers to the activation of unconscious material in the therapist's psyche, evoked by the client and his or her dynamics and material. (Courtois, 1993). We must acknowledge and explore our own vulnerability during the therapeutic process. Such vulnerability leaves us susceptible to developing significant countertransference responses. Having a supervisory relationship either with peers or individually will aid in this effort. A willingness to explore these responses is built on the acceptance that we are affected by the work, and that the impact is triggered by the "stories" we are told.

Conceptually, there are three types of negative countertransference reactions to working with survivors: *avoidance, attraction*, and *attack* (Renshaw 1982).

Avoidance refers to the desire to deny, escape from, or not see the situation as it really is. It is generally based on such emotions as anxiety, discomfort, repugnance, dread, and/or horror. The therapist who routinely fails to ask a client about any incest or abuse history during the assessment stage of the therapeutic intervention would seemingly be avoiding the possible response, and thus his own discomfort in addressing the issues.

At the initial assessment of a client referred to me (Mark) when her current therapist had left the area, I inquired about her prior treatment experience. Andrea had been in therapy with her previous therapist for six years. She recalled that they had had a wonderful relationship, able to talk about anything. As she had identified herself to me as a survivor of incest, I asked about her therapy and her understanding of her incest history, as well as the current stage or progress of her recovery from the trauma. Andrea gave me an inquisitive look, and stated the incest had not been addressed during all those years of therapy. She recounted that at the beginning of the treatment process she had broached the subject of her abuse on several occasions, but the therapist never directly, or even indirectly, addressed it with her. Andrea interpreted this perceived lack of interest or discussion as an indication that the therapist did not view her abuse as a significant issue or relevant to her current life situation. Since she had assumed that the therapist knew what was best for her, she disregarded the issue as well. As her current treatment process began, Andrea found it extremely difficult and anxiety provoking to have any dialogue concerning her abuse, its impact on her current life situations, or discussion of any family history. At that point, she decided to terminate therapy. She only returned months later when she realized that she needed to confront this issue in order to move on with her life.

As we know, many clients do not freely offer their history of abuse, and present for therapy with a wide variety of other symptoms and complaints. On an unconscious level, when the question of abuse is raised initially, it offers the client the message that it is "safe and acceptable" to discuss this information and that the information and material will be heard. However, because of the traumatic issues involved with this kind of abuse, it creates the greatest level of discomfort in therapists who tend to react to such a story with avoidance.

I (Mark) remember watching a supervision tape of a young therapist I will call Debby who was conducting an interview with an incest survivor named Ruby. Ruby had come to therapy to gain a better understanding of what happened to her. As she was "telling her story," Debby was quite unconsciously shaking her head, with her hand holding her face. What does this kind of body language say to the client? The potential for misreading the meaning of this reaction is great. The implicit message may be that it isn't safe to tell the story in this room. The therapist's apparent discomfort could further unsettle a very vulnerable Ruby as she divulges her history.

Asked later about the reactions she was having as Ruby told her story, Debby acknowledged her discomfort, but stated that she was unaware of shaking her head, or putting her hand to her face. Continued supervision and consultation allowed the treatment to progress to an effective resolution. We need to learn the details of the abuse in order to facilitate a greater understanding of the reactions and symptoms that are presented, no matter how disturbing it is. Any attempt on our part to avoid the story implies a dismissal or subtle denial of the abuse's significance.

During another initial interview, Louise presented herself as a survivor of seven years of intra-familial abuse by her father. She explained that she had initially disclosed this abuse to her boyfriend when she was 15 years old. The disclosure resulted in her father being court-ordered into treatment. Mandated to attend, her father took himself and his daughter to therapy. During the first therapeutic interview, the therapist, John, spoke to each party individually. John asked Louise to "tell what happened." She attempted to describe in detail a seven-year history of a progressive sexual relationship with her father. During her retelling of the story, John interrupted her during a particularly difficult part of her recalling the trauma, to tell her that, *"The details are not as significant as the fact that the abuse had stopped."* John then terminated the interview. Even 17 years after that interview, Louise remembers feeling that the therapist *"didn't really care or want to hear about what happened to me."* The therapist then met with the father and daughter together. John told the daughter that what happened *"probably should not have occurred"* and that the best "therapy" would be if *"they would just go home and try to put this behind them."*

Within two weeks of attempting to accommodate her understanding of the therapist's suggestions, and move on with her life, Louise no longer felt safe living with her father. She ran away from home, married a man who was also abusive, and for the next 17 years, Louise thoroughly believed that the abuse was "no big deal," discounting the impact on her life choices. Her defense mechanism was not to address it further.

An extreme example of avoidance is the refusal by one therapist, Bill, to engage in any discussion with the client about his history, even though the client, Jim specifically brought up the issues.

During my (Mark) first session with Jim, he told me about his prior counseling experiences, when he and his third wife had entered into marriage counseling to work on issues that were potentially related to his physical and emotional abuse in this relationship. Jim told me that during the early stages of that therapy, he had asked Bill if the fact that he had been sexually abused by at least two perpetrators could have had anything to do with his current marital difficulties and his anger-management issues. Jim recalled Bill's quick response indicating that there was absolutely no relevant correlation between these two issues.

After giving this response serious thought and seeing his current marriage failing as the other two had done, Jim attempted suicide by ingesting some pills. However, as he was sitting in his car, thinking about his life and circumstance, his gut feelings were "screaming" that he had something to live for, and that his abuse history *was relevant.* Jim went to a local hospital and had his stomach pumped. The following week, he returned to the counselor and recounted what had happened during the suicide attempt. He related how he felt that Bill had discounted his feelings and insights regarding his abuse. Jim remembered Bill's comments that the suicide attempt was ". . . simply a manipulation to get back at his wife because he didn't like something *she* said during the last session. It had nothing to do with not understanding or validating his explanation."

Believing it was unsafe to discuss the incest with this counselor any further, Jim and his wife terminated counseling and continued to consider it on their own. After some difficult dialogue, they both agreed that there was a need to focus on his abuse history before proceeding with any further marital work. After the completion of intensive counseling concerning his sexual abuse, Jim had a better understanding of how this history played a significant role in his view of himself and his intimate relationships. The marital work that followed placed the marriage on much firmer ground.

When a therapist disavows the survivor's emotionality and the perceived significance of abusive histories, he may run the risk of conveying or reinforcing feelings of shame and disgust that the survivor may already carry. The clinician must be careful not to project the belief that the client has been irreparably damaged or tainted because of the abuse, since these attitudes are likely to be parallel to those already held by the survivor.

By maintaining an exaggerated objectivity in the "professional" role, the therapist can distance himself from the client's story in order to defend against intense personal emotions. Unfortunately, such actions can lead to the client's perceiving the therapist's coolness and lack of empathy as a personal rejection, again magnifying already pronounced feelings of inadequacy and self-doubt.

Avoidance can produce guilt feelings when working with survivors that tend to be demonstrated in a variety of ways. Perhaps the therapist might overly identify with the client's pain and suffering. Thus, in the attempt to rescue or protect the client who is perceived as 'fragile,' he may unconsciously avoid discussion of the more difficult and necessary issues involved in the recovery process. There may be guilt feelings in the realization that no one can undo the client's traumatic experiences even by being professional, caring, empathic or concerned. The therapist's task is not to undo the past and deny the pain, but rather to assist the survivor in working through it until it no longer interferes with the ability to function. (Courtois 1988).

Another dimension of the guilt that might impede the therapeutic process occurs when the therapist is acting in the role of surrogate parent. This phenomenon is usually the result of an inadequate exploration of personal history or a lack of understanding of incest dynamics, both of which serve to perpetuate undefined professional roles and boundaries. If the therapist determines that the survivor's recovery is contingent on her repairing or replacing what is perceived as a lack of necessary and appropriate nurturance, she may adapt unhealthy parameters to the relationship.

An extreme example of this dynamic is evident in the case of Janice, an abuse survivor who had been in therapy for several months. Her family of origin had abandoned Janice psychologically and emotionally at the time that she disclosed her abuse. In a misguided effort to be a caring support system, the therapist, Alice, determined that an appropriate treatment would involve her taking the parent's place in this client's life. She then proceeded to introduce Janice to several men (who were also Alice's clients) whom she began to date. Apparently, Alice thought that this was an appropriate strategy to provide socialization for her clients. Eventually, and perhaps predictably, Janice became romantically involved with one of the men and they decided to marry. Delighted, Alice began to assist her in her wedding plans, including lending Janice her (Alice) daughter's wedding dress, and even hosting the wedding at her home. Alice expressed the thought that this action demonstrated that there are people who can be caring and kind, and non-abusive.

Clearly, this therapist has done little of the appropriate exploration of her own motivations for doing survivor/abuse recovery treatment and has clear countertransference issues that need to be resolved.

Attraction is another basic form of problematic countertransference. It connotes a movement toward or desire to become involved in a situation, whereby a therapist may be overly interested in the sexual details of the abuse, perhaps even to the exclusion of the other issues. The client becomes a kind of show, as the therapist derives pleasure from the recounting of the details. As he attempts to satisfy his curiosity, the underlying significance of the story and its impact on the client is pushed to the background.

> A colleague once described having a conversation with another therapist named Clark, who was treating an adolescent survivor of abuse. Clark recounted with heightened interest the events of the abuse. He then casually remarked that he found this case particularly exciting, and assumed that all therapists, (particularly male), at one time or another had imagined what it would be like to be sexually involved with a younger person. The client in this case afforded him the opportunity of hearing such a scenario without actually having to engage in the behavior. Clearly disturbed by these statements, my colleague discussed his concerns with Clark who eventually agreed to transfer the case to another clinician.

Another even more devastating example of such blurring of boundaries is the therapist who actually sexualizes a therapeutic relationship, and rationalizes its benefits for the client. This is rationalized as a "corrective experience," whereby the therapist expresses tenderness and affection towards an abused client that he/she has not received elsewhere. This type of rationale is often very similar to that which the original perpetrator of the abuse used, and it clearly carries the same or even greater risk for long-term negative consequences for the client, to say nothing of the ethical and legal ramifications of such behavior by a professional who should know better.

Whether or not some therapists abuse their roles, gender issues are salient in any discussion of countertransference issues. We must be sensitive to the gender issue regardless of gender of either the therapist or the client. The therapist's implied values and attitudes toward sexual aggression, as well as gender discrimination, may be far more important than whether the therapist is male or female (Dolan, 1991). As a male therapist who has successfully treated a predominantly female caseload, I (Mark) am continually aware of the societal norms or expectations of a man viewed as the more powerful, dominant individual in relationships. This leads to a stereotypical expectation and belief that we often see throughout the literature concerning survivor treatment issues. This is the belief that male therapists can't fully understand the vulnerability, shame and the long term suffering that their female clients have endured, and therefore are unable to adequately identify and empathize with the female survivor's experience. The fact is that none of us, whether male or female, can be in the survivor's skin. Therefore we have to stay intensely curious to discover what the experience was, and exactly how our client suffered. The reverse stereotyped treatment issue of female therapist treating male survivors holds that the difficulty these men have confronting their prior vulnerability and inability to protect themselves, as well as the perceived loss of masculinity, is better addressed by the same gender therapist who can "truly empathize" with them.

A corollary to this existing stereotype held by many women clients presumes that consciously or unconsciously, all male therapists are prone to over-identify with the perpetrator, and thus deny, excuse, or rationalize these behaviors. This needs to be addressed both in the therapy environment with the client as well as outside of it, as therapists explore their own feelings regarding sexuality and the reasons they chose to work with this population. Only then, can we positively identify with clients and assist them by modeling appropriate behaviors or emotional responses between men and women.

In many cases, women survivors will view a male therapist as exploitative and demanding, even while that therapist attempts to convey a message of understanding, compassion and respect.

Consequently, if therapists are fearful of either being rejected or having the client's anger and rage displaced onto them that rightfully belongs with the perpetrator, they may find themselves modifying their intervention in the attempt to impart a message of *"I'm different from all the others"* attempting to make up for the losses that the client has experienced. Some may also overcompensate and take an indulgent, overprotective stance with the survivor that reinforces the survivor's helplessness and recreates yet another situation whereby she becomes dependent and subservient to another man's influence.

The client, on the other hand, may perceive the absence of con-nectedness as evidence of her unworthiness, once again offering an example of her inability to develop satisfying relationships with others.

One can address this issue early when negotiating the thera-peutic contract with a client. I (Mark) directly confront the possible sexual overtones or presumptions by stating that if we do agree to enter into a therapeutic relationship, it will be one where appropri-ate boundaries are set and maintained. The client will be empow-ered with a powerful healing context to counteract and diminish past experiences of mistrust and exploitation.

Although the issue of countertransference that emerges between the male therapist and female survivor has its own implic-it complications, difficulties may also occur with respect to the other therapeutic dyads. When treating female survivors, a woman thera-pist generally will be spared the ordeal of having to deal with the perpetrator issues that confront their male counterparts. However, they may encounter a client's rage at the non-offending parent (usu-ally the mother) who did not provide protection, and who is often viewed as a co-conspirator in the abuse. When confronted with this therapeutic issue, it is important to avoid the reflexive tendency to maintain a psychological distance that may cause clients to feel abandoned. Our role is to assist the client in examining the varied roles, messages, and past relationships as they relate to the mother-daughter relationship.

With respect to a decision to treat either a male or a female sur-vivor, if the perpetrator was female, the clinician's gender may dic-tate the issues encountered. In either scenario, the opportunity exists to provide a genuine corrective learning experience for the client. Men treating clients abused by females may have some of the advantages experienced by women treating clients abused by men (Dolan, 1991). When a female therapist treats a male client, he may have a tendency to attempt to control the therapy session by com-municating in a verbally abusive, discounting, sexist, or sexualizing manner. (Briere, 1989) Such interactions are counter-therapeutic and must be addressed in a fashion that attends to the client's per-ceived vulnerability. Society holds two misperceptions. One is that males are not abused. Ironically, the second is that women cannot abuse young males. It is a direct contradiction to the stereotype of the male as being of the more powerful, sexually aggressive gender. The stereotype as presented by the media is still going strong. From media portrayals in *The Graduate* to *The Freshman*, the idea that it is acceptable for males to be introduced to *sex* at an early age is promoted repeatedly. This is a confusing and complex message that male survivors carry into the treatment process, and it needs to be debunked or discounted.

The last of Renshaw's types of negative countertransference is that of *Attack*, which is motivated by anger and condemnation of the activity and connotes aggressive responses to those involved with it. When a therapist respectfully listens to a client's abuse history, he will frequently have feelings of anger, rage, indignation and disgust in response to this story. We have ascribed to ourselves a desire to help others and to right injustices whenever possible. It is natural for us to have angry feelings toward the perpetrator, other family members, and the societal forces that allowed this injustice to occur. Utilizing a modeling mechanism can be helpful to our clients as we acknowledge our feelings about what happened to them. We must proceed carefully, so as not to project onto clients an assumption as to how or when they should feel the same anger or rage about the abuse. If the therapist expresses these emotions prematurely, he may convey a message that he is angry with the client. The therapeutic work would have to take a detour while the clinician explains or rationalizes personal feelings, assuming that he has observed and properly assessed the client's response.

Consequently, if and when we feel intense rage as a response to the abuse our client has shared with us, it is best processed outside of the therapy setting through clinical and/or peer supervision, or if necessary, our own therapy.

We must continue to maintain appropriate awareness of the potential for the projection of rage or other negative emotions onto the client. The need to "prove we care" may elicit fear or rageful responses in ourselves when we believe that we should be seen by our clients as trustworthy and nurturing. Any evidence of our inability to tolerate a client's rage, or negative reactions, or to understand and cope with our own parallel feelings, ultimately can lead to the perception of our rejection of the client, perhaps resulting in a premature termination from therapy.

The therapist is not the parent and cannot make up for past losses. Clients must grieve for their losses. While therapists may be traumatized doing this work. Therapists must decline being another sadistic abuser. (Caloff, 1987)

In summary, therapists bring many issues and emotions related to the perceptions of themselves, their beliefs, insecurities and prior experiences into the therapy process when dealing with incest or abuse survivors. While engaged in this process, we must strive to arrive at a balanced perspective within the treatment.

Inherent with an understanding of the issues of countertransference, we must also learn how to take appropriate care of ourselves with regard to how this type of work affects us. The next section in this chapter highlights the issues of self-care for the therapists and a discussion of how we must take special precautions to foster awareness and to handle the impact of this work on our own cognitive constructs and belief systems.

SELF-CARE: AMELIORATION OF SECONDARY TRAUMA

A student social worker that I (Mark) had supervised was asked to write her impressions of an adolescent incest survivor with whom she was working. Part of her process recording was:

> I really enjoyed working with S., but during our time together, I frequently found myself, when I was away from the office, thinking about her and the terrible things that had happened to her. I had nightmares on more than one occasion, I seemingly suspected every man I saw with children as a prospective perpetrator and I became increasingly, and dare I say, paranoid about their safety and the safety and well-being of my own small children. I found myself getting irritable and distracted, and even questioned relationships that had previously been satisfactory. I really didn't know what was happening to me . . . until I spoke about it to other students having similar experiences. We all recognized the necessity to get "grounded" on a regular basis. . . .

The feelings and perceptions that this student is expressing are common phenomena experienced among the clinicians treating abuse survivors. The terms "secondary post-traumatic stress," or "vicarious traumatization" (McCann & Peariman) or "contact victimization" (Courtois) have been used to describe the significant phenomenon which occurs, and are viewed as psychological consequences for therapists exposed to traumas experienced by their clients. As discussed further in Chapter 5, when treating abuse survivors we are expected to hear, accept and validate the client's story. While processing the sensitive information being expressed by our clients, and in making competent clinical evaluations, judgments

and interventions, we must also objectively monitor our own countertransference issues that are encountered during the session. We
thus give ourselves the ability to remain respectfully and appropriately objective, while still acknowledging and validating the client's
experiences. There is a consistent level of emotionality involved as
clients tell these stories. Few other treatment populations require
that therapists utilize the clinical relationship to provide the client
with both the necessary emotional containment and the facilitation
of the requisite emotional discharge, as well as the resolution of
traumatic material. This resolution involves breaking through the
habitual patterns of numbing, denial or abreacting; and moving into
accepting events and losses, grieving, and making new sense or
meaning of the victimization that we assist the client in achieving.
(Chu, 1990)

Any clinician who is deeply concerned and caring about his
clients appears to be at risk for experiencing symptoms of traumatization by hearing how another vulnerable person has been severely
hurt. (Dolan, 1991) As these symptoms surface, they frequently
leave the therapist feeling irritable, "burned out," in despair, hope-
less, and even incompetent. It is at that juncture, that our clinical
colleague begins to feel emotional and physical fatigue. He can find
himself dreading the therapy hour, or sustaining an undue fascina-
tion and focus with the content rather than the process of therapy.
Some therapists report "physiological empathy," a somatization in
response to the unconscious mirroring of the client's physiology.

These reactions make us more vulnerable than other clinicians.
While hearing the clients' stories is imperative, continuing to assist
in their recovery will frequently stimulate significant amounts of
unconscious material, which proves uncomfortable for us. We may
even experience discomfort in the form of secondary symptoms of
post-traumatic stress. These may include sleeplessness, a vivid mental replaying of the client's description of the trauma (flashbacks), a
lack of interest in experiences that previously offered pleasure or the
inability to enjoy life (anhedonia), loss of humor and the ability to
play, "numbing," and generalized anxiety similar to that found in
actual victims of sexual trauma. Nightmares are common for those
therapists experiencing secondary post-traumatic stress.

One of the keys to preventing or managing secondary traumatization is to maintain clear boundaries between personal and professional activities. Much of the psychological distress that therapists experience is the shattering of some of the basic assumptions
we all hold concerning the world in which we live in. Survivors

believe that the world continues to be unsafe for them in the present even though the original conditions have ceased to exist. This increases their sense of vulnerability in the world. No longer can they believe the adage of "good things happen to good people" when they report the dismantling of their basic assumptions, values and beliefs about existential safety inside the family unit that parents and family were expected to afford to their offspring.

Mental health professionals who believe that they have some control over the direction of their own lives, and possess the capacity to impact the lives of their client often find it difficult to accept the fact that their intention, motivation and capability to help others is not always validated by a just and fair world. Confronting this reality can be disheartening and frightening because it forces us to acknowledge our own vulnerability. Feelings such as these may generate expressions of indifference, detachment, and loss of faith in humanity's ability to care for their children appropriately, causing free-floating anger and resentment in the therapist. We must take care not to displace anger and detachment onto the survivor. Those feelings must be resolved outside the therapy room.

> The therapist who does not work through their (sic) own struggles or existential crisis, runs the risk of not being able to hear a client's deepest struggles. This may result in the therapist's avoiding some of the more painful abreactive work, consciously or unconsciously, or the therapist may try to alleviate or fix the client's pain for their own comfort . . . It is essential that the therapist hold onto their own ontological security—to be safely in a world that has meaning and hope. The hopelessness, cynical or frightened therapist will be unable to hold any hope for the client's recovery- an essential, albeit intangible, part of the therapeutic process. (Steele & Colrain, 1990).

Inherent in the treatment of survivor clients is the realization that they can be quite needy, and thus, tap into our very nurturing capacities and strategies. When therapists fall prey to the traps of malleable boundaries, they don't hold true to their basic beliefs and values which should transcend their client's circumstances. We intensify our difficulties as we vacillate between these inherent values and wanting to meet our clients' needs. The remedy is to set essential limits and appropriate boundaries and acknowledge the potential countertransference. It is an impediment to successful therapy when a clinician ignores signs of referred post-traumatic stress symptoms.

Examining one's level of stress and possible over-commitment to the therapeutic recovery process will prevent many of these problems. The questionnaire, which is included in Appendix B, will help assess what vulnerabilities and boundaries issues might exist for you. They are designed as a self-assessment quiz. While there is no right or wrong answer to any question, putting these questions in the forefront of your mind will be helpful. The content ranges from how you decide the kinds of clients to work with to how you set limits to allow you to take care of yourself. Just by asking yourself the questions and really thinking through the answers, you will have a clearer understanding of what your personal boundaries are, and how you respect them in your practice of counseling.

If these questions do not arouse feelings or an internal dialogue/debate within yourself, you run the risk of allowing your countertransference to go unchecked. This self-appraisal and an understanding of the issues highlighted by these questions can help you challenge your behavior and reduce resentful, withholding, or punitive feelings. If you ignore the need to set and maintain your personal boundaries, you may possibly recreate boundary violation scenarios for the client.

Maintaining your appropriate boundaries such as treasuring vacation time, respecting time commitments, and taking care of personal needs models appropriate behavior for clients who have very few models. Continually experiencing blurred boundaries between you and your clients may cause stress for you, as you risk confusing your own needs with those of your clients. One of the caveats for doing this work is that you only work as hard as the client does, and make certain that the client takes most of the responsibility for the outcome of the therapy. Failure to follow these guidelines may relegate you to the role of caretaker and diminishing your potential as healer. To proceed on this path most certainly guarantees frustration and resentment for you and a propensity toward "learned passivity" and disempowerment for your client. If you believe that your clients are strong enough to process whatever information and insight you offer because they have survived the abuse, you may be in danger of "pushing" the therapy at a faster pace than clients may tolerate. "Starting where the client is" and pacing the speed and duration of the therapy process remains vitally important to a successful outcome.

When you begin to notice your own signals of secondary post-traumatic stress, you need to separate yourself from being anchored into the emotional triggers of the trauma work, and partake in experiences that generate hope and comfort. This "separator state" is as simple as it is important. By simply changing your clothing when you come home from work, you will experience a distance from the tension. Try an activity as easy as taking the dog for a walk, spending time playing with your child, reading your favorite non-professional magazine or newspaper. For those so inclined, a physical workout will relieve or sweat out the stress. Develop a ritual that signals to you that "My day is done, work is complete, and *its time for me!*" The variety of rituals to relieve the stressors that this work produces is as varied as the personality style of the therapist. Yvonne Dolan comments concerning rituals:

> *Do not underestimate their importance.* Rituals provide boundaries between work and non-work. This is due to the psychologically compelling aspects of working with trauma, which the unconscious is likely to respond to all too thoroughly. Fortunately, the unconscious will respond also to these rituals. (Dolan, 1991, p.222)

A therapist informed me about his ritual for separating each day from work. In order for this therapist, to return to his home each evening, he had to drive his car across a bridge. Each evening, before he left his office, he would gather up all of the "garbage" he had accumulated that day, put it in a bag, and just before he was about to drive across the bridge, he would stop, and "throw away the day's garbage." This ritual allowed him to return home unburdened, able to enjoy his evening.

Another possibility is to recognize that your desk, fax, office, etc will be there in the morning. Stay conscious of your thoughts and actions so as you clear your desk and put things away for the evening, you "put away" the stress of the day. When you lock the desk or door to your office, you form another barrier. As you leave the building, and hear or see the door shut behind you, notice the release of stress as you leave it in that building. Begin looking forward to your free time at home and imagine activities you enjoy there. As you travel to your home, make these positive thoughts stronger and these images brighter. When you program these rituals into your life, you will empower yourself to regenerate your energies.

Focus on personal hobbies, (crafts or collections) sports; such as tennis, golf or swimming, small pleasures like doing crossword puzzles or watching your favorite show on TV, as well as important interpersonal connections and relationships which inspire, encourage or excite you. Get involved in community activities or service clubs which accomplish objectives in improving the quality of life for your fellow citizens.

Additionally, I (Jill) remind myself of how very fortunate I am to have grown up in a loving, safe home, feeling very protected and nurtured by both my parents, as well as married to a loving and considerate man. Truly appreciating one's own blessings helps put all the problems and trauma's that clients are coping with into a proper perspective.

In conclusion, if therapists are truthful with themselves regarding the significance of secondary post-traumatic stress and its impact on their daily lives, they would continually self-assess, seek out networking, both professional and collegial supervisory opportunities on a regular basis to vent emotions, look at treatment concerns, and to examine their work. We must take the opportunity to assess feelings and concerns that arise with respect to self-care whenever we work with the substance and fallout of trauma. Giving the proper attention to the feelings and reactions we are experiencing, we can more easily and successfully depotentiate the effects of that traumatic work, get past it, and learn to lead more productive, healthy and fulfilling lives. This is the same advice that we give our ailing clients. It is vital that we take it ourselves.

[2]

Replaying the Tapes

Survivor Belief Systems

Problems will always be with us. The problem is not the
problem; the problem is the way people cope. This is what
destroys people, not the problem. Then when we learn to
cope differently, we deal with the problem differently, and
they become different.

—Virginia Satir.

Regardless of the current circumstances which exist in our lives,
a vast number of the decisions we make, and the reasons we
make them are directly related to our earlier experiences. We frequently decide what to do or what to say and how to say it based on
cognitions of these earlier experiences and interactions as well as
their perceived outcomes. These interactions and experiences are
not always positive and often skew our life choices and decisions to
ostensibly protect ourselves from projected future dangers.
Survivors of sexual abuse, particularly, predicate their decision making on those negative experiences and emotions that filter and distort their perceptions of reality regarding their self-esteem and self-
worth. How they feel about themselves and their childhood experiences is reflected and "acted out" by their responses and feelings in
the present.

This chapter discusses many of these negative experiences, feelings and responses as well as how these experiences translate into
"themes" which clients present to us for treatment. A better understanding of these cognitive distortions, how they are modeled in the
client's daily functioning and some suggestions about how to chal-

21

lenge these limiting beliefs offers the therapist additional tools to assist in the rebuilding of the client's self-esteem and self-worth.

Survivors of childhood sexual abuse are likely to suffer negative effects in how they perceive and understand themselves, others, and the future. (Briere, 1989; McCann, Pearlman, Sackhiem, & Abramson, 1985; Dolan, 1991) These perceptual distortions are also known as "cognitive effects" (Briere, 1989) in that they relate to thinking as opposed to feeling. These distortions become themes of limiting beliefs which impact them throughout their lives and present significant and pertinent treatment issues in therapy. These belief systems embed themselves in the impact of the abuse trauma and demonstrate the long-term effects of the abuse. We will discuss the following themes in the treatment of abuse victims and present strategies of how to help them develop more effective and more empowering beliefs.

1. Guilt and shame
2. Self-esteem or negative self-affirmation
3. Grief and loss
4. Anger
5. Interpersonal /intimacy issues
6. Codependency
7. Sexuality
8. Self-destructive behaviors
9. Dissociation

GUILT AND SHAME

Adult survivors of incest manifest feelings of guilt and shame so often that we consider it an almost universal response. This theme recurs frequently on a variety of levels within the therapeutic process (Sanderson, 1995). Guilt occurs when one believes he has violated his own standards of ethics, morals and values. A major component in feelings of guilt is "that the survivor, regardless of the reality of the actual abuse situation, feels themselves responsible for their incest experience" (Sanderson, 1995). They would tend to focus on their contribution to the abuse rather than believe that another family member (the abuser) is at fault. Guilt usually enables one to take responsibility for actions, make amends, learn from the experience and move on. It is not helpful in situations where the person experiencing it is not at fault. These feelings of guilt become so integrated into the self that they frequently influence other situations in which the child, and later the adult, assumes responsibility for situations in which there is no personal responsibility or that are not within their control. The survivor continues to feel guilty when *anything* goes wrong. Shame is a pervasive, painful feeling that clients feel when they have "not measured up" to someone else's standards; that they are bad, worthless, and insufficient in another's estimation. It is a function of feeling judged.

Survivors frequently live with the responsibility of keeping the abuse secret from others on behalf of the family. Because they cannot share their story, the feelings of being bad become even more intense, manifesting itself in feelings of rejection and disgust with one's self.

Some survivors have ambivalent feelings toward the offender, particularly when the offender provided nurturance and affection that was otherwise lacking. It makes it difficult to accept the enormity of the violation. A survivor's protectiveness of the perpetrator may also be due to the role reversal or "parentification" she experienced, coupled with an overdeveloped sense of responsibility and protection. (Courtois, 1988) We can assist the victims in understanding that the responsibility for the abuse lies with the perpetrator.

Feelings of intimacy or sexual arousal associated with the abuse compound the confusion and sense of guilt for the survivor. Frequently this admission is excruciating for the client. We need to educate and reassure our clients about the physical role of sexual arousal as an independent response that is in no way indicative of complicity or wrongdoing. It can also be understood as a way their body coped with the abuse experience, a way of blocking out the fear, confusion, emotional and possibly physical pain. McDonald, Lambie & Simmonds (1995) suggest asking whether the client would have chosen to have the arousal experience in those circumstances. Once the client acknowledges that they would not have chosen it, the therapist can better clarify the distinctions. The body was responding to circumstances over which it had no control. By re-attributing responsibility for the abuse and addressing associated guilt feelings, issues of shame can be appropriately resolved.

Cristina, at the age of thirty-two, entered treatment to address issues related to a series of failed and unsatisfactory relationships. She spoke of how all of her relationships initially seemed to revolve around her ability to attract all men sexually. "They never seem to be interested in me for anything else." The relationships never lasted, and Cristina was concerned that she might never have a meaningful relationship.

During the early stages of treatment, Cristina had revealed that she had been sexually abused by both her mother's boyfriend and one of his friends, starting at age ten and continuing until age fifteen, when she left home. Cristina had confidence, that she could have prevented the abuse in her early teens if she had wanted to. However, she claimed that the reason she allowed the abuse to continue for such a prolonged period was a sense of "gratitude" her mother seemed to transmit to her. On one occasion, when her mother had decided that she no longer wanted to date a certain man, she let Cristina know that he was "available," and encouraged her daughter to begin a more active, open relationship with him, offering Cristina the opportunity to share her bedroom with him, since the man was unemployed and had no place to stay. If Cristina was involved in sexual relationships with these men, then her mother was relieved of her obligation.

Although she never confronted her mother with this perception, she remained clear with herself that in a specific way, she was able to "keep peace in the house" which also made life easier for her siblings who would not have to be subjected to fights between mother and boyfriend.

With regard to her relationships with peer-age boys, Cristina was aware that she could get boys to do whatever she needed or wanted, as long as the prospect of a sexual interaction was available. It seemed to be her only source of power or acceptance. She stated that her sexuality was all she had to offer to people. However, she admitted that no relationship lasted very long, and that she always viewed herself in a negative way because of her inability to maintain any relationships, *"I always felt I didn't try hard enough, especially when the sex was not enough to keep us going."*

In the early stages of our work together, Cristina acknowledged that her adult choice in men usually was dictated by whether or not the man was dependent enough to fulfill her need to control the relationship. For her the choices were logical and predictable. Her disproportionate need for control involved controlling the focus, flow and intensity of each therapy session. She would dictate the level of disclosure she was willing to share regarding her history. When I (Mark) did not pressure Cristina past her comfort point that she defined, she began to trust the collaborative relationship and an important therapeutic alliance was established. In time, she responded to this increased trust and comfort level by verbalizing her sense of betrayal and anger she felt toward her mother for using her as a "pawn" to shield the mother from having to deal with these boyfriends directly.

I encouraged Cristina to discuss this anger, as well as her ambiguity and confusion about sex, her need to be in control, and ultimately, her true desire for affection and nurturance, not only from the men in her life, but from people in general.

I invited her to "experiment" by considering all the different types of men and relationships that exist in the world. What would happen if when she went on a date and was enthused to be with the person, she refused a sexual encounter? As she applied a new filter to her perception of how other men treated women they loved and cared about, she came to the realization that there could indeed be relationships where men could be affectionate, caring and considerate, but not have it turn sexual. She thought about friendships with young women she had made in her years of school which were not based on sexuality or favors. She was able to "put to rest" her inability to sustain relationships with men and women. She came to understand that her desire for affection, nurturance, and approval, things she was never able to gain from her family of origin, did not necessitate sexual relations and that she had more to contribute to a relationship than her sexuality. When treatment ended she was still searching for "Mr. Right," but was no longer desperate to please someone unconditionally.

SELF-ESTEEM OR NEGATIVE SELF-AFFIRMATION

Self-esteem is essential for psychological survival. It is a sense of self-evaluation and assessment that influences and controls the degree of confidence and contentment with oneself. A sense of self-esteem is based on life experiences that include family messages, personal achievements, relationships and even the lessons learned from our mistakes.

All survivors of abuse have distortions in their sense of self-esteem. It is likely to be an even greater problem for those who have been told by their abuser or by others, that they were in some way responsible. There are persistent feelings of inadequacy and emptiness, or the inability or even fear of asserting oneself or taking risks. The poor self-esteem is then exacerbated and reinforced by a tendency to notice their own failures, and to ignore any successes that are inconsistent with their negative view of themselves. Poor self-esteem can become so deeply entrenched that, even when exposed to positive experiences, it becomes extremely difficult for the survivor to validate their positive attributes or accomplishments.

When working with survivors, it is important to explore the negative messages that the survivor has internalized. We can help the client discover the origins and present importance of these internal negative introjects. One of the most effective means of intervening is to cognitively challenge and enunciate consciously what is happening at a subliminal level. We focus on:

- Who generated these messages? In whose voice do they hear them inside?
- How were these messages transmitted?
- When did they first notice that the messages existed, and what understanding do they have about their personal vulnerability to these messages? What emotional buttons are the messages pushing?
- What importance (if any) do these messages still hold for the survivor?

As the psychotherapy process explores these issues, we can encourage the client to reevaluate and examine the messages and become more objective about their veracity, accuracy and relevance. We educate the client about the issues brought on by the abuse, and about how the client's nuclear family dynamics, belief systems and internal messages contribute to the client's current sense of self. The client can better understand how these negative messages had been conveyed at a time when a child's cognitive and logical developmental level was inadequate to fully understand and process the messages. Combined with the concomitant psychological distortions, they go unchallenged by fact and circumstance. When a child internalizes these implicit messages, he integrates them into his self-image. The negative belief continues into his adult self-image, unaltered. Once a client is aware of the negative messages that were internalized, he develops an intense need to make sense of the abusive situation and the fallout from it. It is important to teach the client to test the reality basis for these messages and make a decision to discard the negative thoughts that are based on confusion and manipulations.

When Mary initially entered treatment, she was a 35-year-old business executive, who had been aware of her sexual abuse experiences, but had never entered into a therapeutic relationship to examine the possible effects of the abuse on her functioning. Although quite successful in her business environment, she seemed to rely on the belief that she "was in the right place, at the right time." Attributing her accomplishments to luck or circumstances, she found it difficult to accept compliments or to find any validation in her success that could possibly be attributed to a level of competence rather than good fortune.

Mary's entrance into therapy was precipitated by two concurrent realities with which she found herself confronted. The first was that she was about to be offered a promotion to a position she did not feet competent to take. When asked to describe why she felt she was being considered for the promotion, she proffered no positive portrayal of herself, but saw her "true self" as indecisive, unimaginative, and unable to focus clearly on a task.

The second dilemma was that a colleague whom she had admired from afar, asked her to go to a concert with him. She was now questioning his "sanity" about his wanting to go out with someone as unattractive, uninteresting, and shallow an individual as she was.

As treatment began, Mary's negative image and belief about her current self was in direct correlation to the emotions she felt during the time of her abuse by her stepfather. During that period, she saw herself as someone who couldn't satisfy or please people, "never good enough," and she believed she was powerless to alter people's perceptions of her. Not only had Mary's mother been continually critical of both her appearance and behavior, the overt animosity toward her daughter clearly escalated as the abuse began.

Further complicating her self-image was that as Mary internalized her mother's criticism, she found it incongruous that her stepfather would focus his attention on her, despite her physical "shortcomings."

Therapy began as we focused her attention on the positive qualities and assets that had allowed her to succeed in achieving her professional objectives. It was interesting to note that she identified many personal qualities that she could admit to liking about herself. She was assigned the task of interviewing friends and colleagues to find out what it was that they admired and respected about her. She began a list of these qualities. She was then asked to recall those relevant behaviors that she could associate with that long list of qualities. In the face of this irrefutable evidence, the negative belief began to diminish in intensity and the extent of its influence on her life. We reframed the current relevance of the hypnotic messages and binds her family placed on her, as well as their impact on her current level of functioning,

Mary spent considerable time exploring and accepting her talents, attributes, and achievements. She began to develop a "sense of competence and importance." This was in marked contrast to her initial "right place, right time" belief as the rationale for her personal and professional successes. She was able to consistently view herself more objectively. She also realized there were things about herself that would not always please her or others. By re-evaluating her negative self-image, challenging her internalized distorted belief system and perceptions, as well as allowing herself to acknowledge the positive aspects about herself, she was able to integrate all of her characteristics into a more balanced and realistic self-image. She accepted the promotion and flourished in it. She dated the man a few times and was pleasantly surprised to recognize he was "not my type!" and to feel OK about it.

GRIEF AND LOSS

Grieving and mourning the losses connected to the survivor's abuse are a necessary part of the therapeutic process. Because many survivors do not recognize a need to grieve and have no permission or knowledge of how to express that grief, they adapt to their reality by simply trying to put the past to rest. It is important for us to support and encourage these survivors to take a period of planned mourning to identify, acknowledge, and grieve their multiple losses. The most common losses include: innocence and trust, a normal childhood, spontaneity, a neglect of the inner child, a family system that should have protected them, as well as the ability to experience joy and fun.

Grieving, although necessary, remains extremely difficult for many survivors. They deny themselves the permission and the right to express their sadness, sorrow, or any emotionality. Part of it may be that if they ignore these emotions, they believe the problem will "die of neglect." Another reason for this state of denial is that in their family of origin, expressions of emotions were considered inappropriate, unjustified or were admonished. The messages to "put it behind you," or "forget about it" carry a great deal of weight when one is attempting to express any emotionality appropriate to grief. Old guilt reactions are often triggered and are uncomfortable to handle. Survivors may express the belief that things are getting worse, or that they are regressing as they get in touch with the many grief responses that they are experiencing. We can normalize these feelings and appropriately reframe them as a necessary and important part of the healing process.

Crying is particularly hard for these clients, as they believe that their crying is seen as weakness. This is particularly true among male clients, where societal expectations tell them to "be strong." The old adage of "big boys don't cry" is a value that resounds in many male clients as they become aware of the losses they have suffered as a result of their abuse. In the clinical setting, some therapists may view sadness and tears in men as "a sign of self-pity and are intolerant of it, preventing their clients from fully grieving their losses . . ." (Hunter, 1990, pg. 87)

Regardless of gender, crying is viewed as vulnerability and the client may be afraid that if they do cry, no one will listen or understand. Another general fear about expressing appropriate grief by crying is that "if they begin to cry, they might not be able to stop." Sanderson (1995) used the analogy of tears as being useful in the "cleaning of the incest wound," as if tears can prevent further infection of the wound. While the therapist and any of the client's supportive friends can provide a salve for the wounds, the survivor, himself, needs to cleanse them with tears before the 'salve' can be applied.

Different cultures and experiences make it important that we remain flexible and reject dogmatism of any kind in treating our clients. There are times when we must respect a client's unique style of responding to the world and creatively develop interventions in collaboration with the client to get more effective results.

Rachel's father had sexually abused her for several years during her childhood. While she was in treatment, it became obvious that, remembrances of her childhood experiences occasionally brought her to the verge of tears. She would allow one, maybe two to fall onto her cheek, but no more. "I can't cry, I have never cried in my entire life. My mother has told me that even when I hurt myself as a child, I would not cry."

Rachel's memories of her nuclear family dynamics were continual reminders of how crying or losing control of any emotions was not acceptable. She observed her mother being hit by Rachel's father if she disagreed with him. An implicit message which was repeated again and again was that even as the molestation continued, she could be seen, but she was not to be heard. She learned that her emotions were to be hidden and therefore she was never exposed to her father's wrath.

In addition to several other group members, I continued to reassure her that crying would not be expressing weakness or vulnerability, but rather courage and strength. They redefined crying as a form of emotional release and cleansing that allows healing to occur. Although she intellectually acknowledged that she certainly could and would stop crying, all the reassurance and group support was to no avail. Rachel never openly cried, either during therapy sessions, or at home, as she continued to work toward her recovery. In the framework of collaboration, the group had to design alternative ways of expressing grief and letting go that would give Rachel some sense of being in control and moving on.

One intervention was to have Rachel step into the imaginary role of a prosecutor and write a therapeutic "letter" of indictment to the abuser explaining in great detail what he had done to rob her of her innocence, trust, and appropriate childhood fun. This generated a great deal of energy and a sense of outrage which helped her move out of helplessness.

The next task was to invite Rachel to step into the role of an "advocate" for the younger self, and write down all the negative responses she had experienced over the years ranging from the silliest fantasies, such as the idea that the abuser would "fall into a pit of hot lava, never to return," to the most negative internal messages such as "you're nothing." These were to be laid figuratively at the feet of her abuser in an attempt to give back the "hand-me-down" messages that she had been saddled with over the years. When she found the task of writing these negative messages difficult, she thought of creating a collage which represented these negative imprints. She actually enjoyed going through magazines to find pictures which expressed these concepts to some parts of her unconscious. She was given plenty of permission that the collage did not need to make sense to anyone but her. She added to the picture by drawing with a large box of crayons to express things she could not find in a magazine. Rachel could articulate that she was "haunted" by the memories of her father's abuse, not only of her but the treatment of her mother. These memories had blocked the expression of emotions related to sadness or losses for as she described, the *"fear of feeling the feelings was better than confronting the terrible senses of letting go of the power my father still holds"* these many years later. Toward the end of her treatment, Rachel began to let go of some of those "fears of feeling" and could bring herself to shed those rare tears without worrying that she would be unable to stop. She reported that she was feeling more at peace with herself and believed she had put an end to that traumatic portion of her life.

ANGER

The subject of anger is one that comes up at various stages of the treatment process. Survivors differ greatly in their response to their abuse. Anger is often one of the most difficult affective responses to deal with during therapy. It is a normal and natural response to the violation which was experienced.

The survivor needs to understand that controlled anger is an appropriate response which has more energy attached to it than the lethargic helplessness engendered by guilt, shame or grief, and is frequently a response to those feelings. Learning how to cope with anger and allow its healthy expression is often a formidable task, but one that will be a powerful, healthy and much deserved release. It may be the first time that they have felt a sense of power since the abuse. It is a sign that they have taken a significant step away from the role of "victim," that they are beginning to take charge of their lives, and that the abuse is losing some of its power to affect them. (MacDonald, 1995)

Our ability to provide a safe environment through building a therapeutic alliance can encourage a helpful discharge of anger. Because many survivors believe anger *always* has powerful negative consequences, it is important to help them explore the concept that anger is a positive, healthy emotion and is a totally appropriate response to a history of sexual abuse.

As they experience the beneficial aspects of using this discharge as a release of tension, these clients can validate these normal and appropriate feelings, and understand their anger to be an important signal that their personal values and standards have been violated. It is also important to explore the intrinsic meaning that anger has for the survivor, as well as to establish its source.

Societal norms, faulty value systems as well as childhood experiences inside the nuclear family correlate with the level and ease of anger expression among survivors. Women tend to carry a pervasive stigma against anger in the same way men have been taught that crying is not permitted. They don't know how to handle this troubling emotion in culturally acceptable ways. Women are taught specifically to not express their anger and outrage, perhaps because it is not "ladylike" or they may confuse anger with violence. Since women tend to internalize anger, they exhibit more symptoms of depression which is 'internalized anger.' Men, on the other hand, are told to "be a man" or "let it out" and are more likely to externalize that anger toward others. As noted earlier, men have similar limitations in finding acceptable ways to express grief and sadness.

As we educate our clients and validate all these intense reactions as normal responses to their abnormal experiences, we may want to acknowledge that a client's fear to express any anger is equally understandable, much like fearing the intense emotion of crying. Although the client has previously "held onto" or buried their anger for fear of being in an uncontrollable rage, they need to know that a healthy expression of their anger is desirable and appropriate. In keeping with our framework of collaboration, creating alternative effective behaviors often are necessary.

Although twenty-nine years old, Sarah stated that she had never raised her voice throughout her life. She always had been taught to keep control of her emotions, and to act "lady-like." During the course of individual and group treatment, as Sarah effectively confronted her history and intellectually verbalized the anger she felt toward both her father who had abused her, and her mother, who had not protected her, she was still unable to scream or raise her voice. She wanted to change the tension and depression she felt inside her body, and agreed that if she could physically express the internal angst, she would feel better. The metaphor that we used was ingesting spoiled food and needing to throw up to rid the body of poisons which were upsetting the internal balance. We spent some time acknowledging the positive intentions of that internal part of her that valued being in control, but were now inhibiting her capability to free herself from repression. I (Mark) watched her struggle in vain to allow a raised tone to emerge from her mouth. Sarah was nearing the completion of what she deemed as successful therapy, in spite of her inability to raise her voice. As the last session was approaching, she stated, "Last night, I think I felt something—I think it's coming . . ." As the final group session was winding down, Sarah recounted her struggles to "vent herself," and stated "now I think it's ready" and with that, came forth the loudest, most gut wrenching scream of anguish and anger that lasted at least thirty seconds. After she was done, she regained her passive posture, took a deep breath, sank back down in the chair, and said quietly, "I feel better now."

We need to draw a clear distinction between what we encourage our clients to do within the therapy context, and what our clients would consider realistic and appropriate coping skills and activities in the contexts in which they live and work. Therapeutic tasks done in the therapy sessions are often metaphors which do not readily translate into appropriate expressions or actions outside of therapy. We operate under the assumption that if our clients are given ample opportunity to fully express, or act out their anger and feelings in the safety of the session; they are less likely to want to act out their anger in an inappropriate way outside. Some survivors become enraged, overtly show their reactions, and then let it go. Others, who are more vulnerable, may feel it inside and continue to deal with it internally by directing the anger against the self. That anger or rage often manifests itself in depression or some kind of self-destructive behaviors such as self-mutilation, eating disorders and suicide attempts. Some even suppress the unacceptable anger until it takes the form of a dissociated identity response so the only way a survivor can deal with the intense emotions of anger or fear is to create an entire personality who somehow has permission to express these emotions. The caution here is to focus on contextually appropriate alternatives relevant to their values and personal ecology which are cooperatively designed and practiced in the session.

Positive anger results in a validation of feelings and an increase in a sense of personal power which is therapeutic for the survivor.

Carol is a 42-year-old whose unhappiness emanated originally from her father's intense anger, and molestation directed against her and two of her three sisters and her mother's inability to recognize it, stop it, or even to comfort her when she was crying. Her experience in school was also traumatic. Kids shunned her, teased her, and she sunk deeper into an intense despondency.

Carol believed she was always on the short end of the family benefits as she experienced both her parents neglecting her interests in favor of other siblings' needs. She broke her engagement to "the only person who treated me like a human being" when her mother strenuously objected to his religion. Because Carol believed it was "wrong" to dishonor her mother and father, she never directed anger against either of her parents. Instead she directed the anger against herself. She was intensely self-critical and took any suggestions or criticism from others personally. When she recalled her father or mother, her facial tonus would become very tight, and her complexion would literally darken. She would start speaking in a deep, loud voice which verbalized hopelessness, blame and guilt. While she blamed her mother for interfering in her life, she felt intense guilt for not standing up for herself. She would bang her head with her hands, distort her face with intense anguish and continue to respond to the world as if these decisions were fresh.

Unfortunately, she married a man who met her mother's approval, but who is a clone of her father in his abusiveness, neglect and disdain of her. Their marital problems replay and reinforce her childhood experiences. She feels trapped because of her economic dependence on his income.

Treatment began slowly, letting Carol complain and vent without censor or negative judgment. I (Jill) began to compliment her on assertively stating what was going on. She was surprised as she thought she was being "evil." When "evil" was reframed as the way she was treated by her father and her husband, and I continued to validate her anger as normal in light of what she experienced, Carol began to let go of the self-blame. When she became "dark with anger," I exaggerated the response and would become even angrier and louder on her behalf, as I modeled yelling at the unfairness of what she had been put through by her father and husband.

In response to her requests for some strategies to cope with these stresses, I offered her the traditional stress management technique of controlled breathing; the cognitive strategy of refuting negative self-talk, not because she had to believe that the refutations were true, but because believing the self-talk was so painful. This paradox seemed to make sense to her at some internal level. After we identified the limiting beliefs which allowed her to maintain this negativity, she was able to formulate a more empowering belief which she began to incorporate. The head banging and self-blaming have stopped. Carol is still married to her husband, but she has started to move toward developing an independent career which may give her enough confidence to move away from him and the continued mistreatment.

INTERPERSONAL AND INTIMACY ISSUES

Interpersonal and intimacy issues are very common themes, which surface throughout the incest or abuse treatment. The survivor's perceived and real impairment with relationships is due to a lack of trust, self-esteem deficits, or "exaggerated relationship needs." (Caruso, 1987) Someone they trusted, who should have protected and cared for them, betrayed these incest survivors. Therefore, it is easier for them to express and understand their inability to trust or share intimacy with others in the present and future. Survivors report that being physically close to someone makes them feel vulnerable and threatened, and that they believe trusting someone will result in being hurt again. Others believe that the only way to get close or intimate with someone is to have sex.

As they enter therapy, survivors have little information or few experiences with healthy relationships. With a resultant inherent lack of trust, survivors fear closeness, and thus destroy their capacity for intimacy to protect against being vulnerable. The client perceives that an abuser perpetuates the relationship for his or her own pleasure and gain, while the survivor's role is to accommodate this need. The fearfulness of engaging with people who might misuse them or abandon them causes survivors to become extra vigilant in their attitudes toward people. It is not unusual for survivors of abuse to purposefully remain distant or unapproachable in relationships or to participate in personal connections that ask little of them, or even to avoid them altogether. Positive self-esteem is a major ingredient in the initiation and maintenance of intimacy. As many survivors struggle with feelings of low self-worth, they internalize and hold onto their concepts of not deserving to be loved, or to enjoy non-abusive relationships. Their choices of partners are frequently based on loneliness and dependency. They may reject or ignore a realistic assessment of the true characteristics of a potential partner in favor of the short term benefits of an attachment of perceived convenience. Survivors expect to receive satisfaction of their many emotional needs and then are intensely disappointed when the relationship cannot give them even the basics necessary to succeed. (Caruso, 1987)

The building of trust within the therapeutic experience can serve as an initial opportunity for the survivor to learn to trust others, which can eventually broaden to other appropriate relationships. We can provide a potent role model to demonstrate that it is possible to trust another person in a way that does not invite exploitation or rejection. A combination of a safe environment, validation, empathy, and support enables the survivor to explore what it means to trust, and to learn that trust does not always precede being hurt or abused. (Sanderson, 1995) In counseling, clients can experience a safe, healthy relationship that has well-defined, appropriate boundaries. They have the opportunity to explore thoughts, feelings and needs with a trustworthy person who can give them skills and strategies in choosing partners wisely and building genuine loving relationships.

Karen was sexually abused by her father for most of her teenage years, and she felt that not only had he abused her, but that she was forever restricted in her ability to form close relationships. While she had had boyfriends throughout her adolescence, she described never being able to feel enough at ease with any of the relationships to establish any level of intimacy. Whenever she came close to establishing potential intimacy with a man she would experience symptoms of panic, followed by severe and prolonged depression. This would precipitate her withdrawing and distancing herself from the relationship and it would quickly end. Karen's fear of intimacy extended to her connections with women. She felt "frightened" and frequently intimidated by women she knew, feeling that she was inferior to them; and had nothing in common. She was certain that on some level, no women were to be trusted. After an initial period of time in individual treatment, where she could begin to experience a trusting relationship with a male therapist, Karen hesitantly agreed to join a survivor's therapy group comprised of men and women, where she found validation and acceptance, and she started to build up trust and respect for the other group members. For the duration of the group, Karen persevered in her new-found determination to form a close bond within the group, including the male members, from whom she found she could seek advice and counsel, concerning her dating experiences.

Upon termination of the group, she had started and maintained a close relationship with two women in the group that has continued for several years. She also remained in contact with the one of the male members, even after he had relocated out of the area.

CODEPENDENCY

Codependency issues are frequent therapy themes for almost all survivors. Codependency, a persistent pattern of learned, self-defeating behaviors, can be devastating as the survivor feels unable to take control of her life. She remains in an obligatory, responsible and/or caretaker role in her relationships. The survivor often adopts a pattern of self-deprecating behavior that is consistently devoid of any acknowledgment of her own feelings or needs. Rather, they tend to place more importance on the needs and feelings of other people ahead of their own appropriate, real needs. They exhibit an indispensable requirement for the approval of others. The survivor adopts the pervasive feeling that there are no choices regarding any of these feelings. She believes that she neither has control over her own life nor is she entitled to it. These learned feelings cause the survivor to seek relationships analogous to those dysfunctional patterns within her own family of origin in which she can continue to take responsibility for the feelings of her family members. This reinforces both the perception of self as a victim and the validity of these intense dependency needs. Many survivors are placed prematurely in the pattern of an adult role, as the "parentified" child, learning to be responsible for the family functioning with little or no expectation that any of her needs will be noticed or responded to.

The reality of this occurrence should come to a surprise of no-one since we all respond to patterns in our life as if it were an implicit assumption that they would continue, in order to maintain a sense of stability, however dysfunctional it is. We can consider the work of Piaget to explain this tendency to repeat patterns. He described children as coming into this world unable to distinguish themselves from anyone else. They and the world are one. Everything is together. There are very diffuse external boundaries. We encourage our children to develop a sense of their own identity, appropriate boundaries and personal uniqueness. We develop a sense of "continuity of self" as we define who we are—and where we belong. (Piaget, J., 1970)

When children have a traumatic experience that intrudes on their sense of self, they begin to feel fragmented and often dissociate from their sense of order, identity and boundary. They become so enmeshed in the dysfunction that they either don't learn appropriate differentiation or are given implicit injunctions against developing an independent identity. As an insightful client remarked, *"It isn't about me as a unique person. It is about what else is going on in the external world, because I feel I have no true self. It is only 'me' in relation to how I impact others. I seem to allow other people to define who I am."*

As an adult, the survivor often takes this kind of experience into her choice of intimate relationships. They may become involved with dependent, immature individuals who want someone to take care of *them*, but who can not reciprocate when the needs of the survivor become known. During the therapy process, the survivor can be assisted in becoming increasingly aware of her own needs and the repeated patterns of care-taking of others. We want her to learn that she deserves to be the recipient of respect and caring and can demand reciprocal consideration in close relationships.

Ashley, age 16, had been sexually abused by her father for seven years. Despite her mother's presence in the home, the relationship between father and daughter had assumed the dynamics of a "happily married couple," with Ashley feeling total responsibility for her father's happiness. With the help of her overly dependent and passive 23 year-old boyfriend, Jack, Ashley disclosed her abuse after she discovered that, despite his promises to the contrary, her father had begun to molest her younger sister.

Throughout her relationship, Ashley had helped Jack emotionally and economically whenever he requested assistance, or when she perceived that he was in need, stating that he had "potential, but needs to be helped along." Shortly after moving out of the family home, Ashley became pregnant. Six weeks into the pregnancy, while she and her boyfriend were preparing to go to their weekly bowling league match, Ashley began to spontaneously miscarry, bleeding profusely. In obvious discomfort and in fear as to what was happening to her, she asked the boyfriend to take her to the hospital. He protested, saying that he really should go bowling, so as not to disappoint their teammates. Ashley agreed with this rationale, and allowed him to leave, while she telephoned and then waited for another friend to take her to the hospital. Although initially resistant as she discussed the situation further, Ashley was finally able to fully hear about how other healthier relationships work so she could re-examine the relationship. Ashley decided to set better limits and boundaries for the continuation of the relationship. The boyfriend ultimately disappointed Ashley several additional times, and Ashley ended the relationship.

We have to emphasize to our clients that they do indeed have strengths, coping mechanisms, resources and capabilities.

SEXUALITY

Sexuality is a common recurring treatment theme which many survivors shy away from, but which is profoundly affected by sexual abuse, and especially incest. It involves the re-introduction of old feelings of coercion, shame, confusion, and pain from the survivor's abusive experiences in their childhood. The survivor feels that she has been damaged sexually through her abuse. As the issues of sexuality are explored within the therapy, survivors often experience those sensations and emotions similar to those felt during the abuse itself. Therefore, although a survivor may desire to engage in adult sexual behaviors, she may find herself unable to put aside these negative feelings. Some of the effects noted with survivors regarding their sexuality are:

- A lack of arousal
- Withdrawal from sexual encounters and interactions
- Sexual orientation and/or identity confusion
- Inability to differentiate affection from sex
- Use of sex as a control mechanism

Lack of arousal or an inability to be sexually intimate is due to a repeated infusion of negative feelings associated with the abuse. During an adult experience of or an attempt to establish intimate sexual relations, the negative feeling overwhelm the survivor, and threaten feelings of arousal; and instead cause feelings of conflict and disgust. It does not take many such experiences before positive, appropriate sexual feelings cease, and a lack of arousal becomes the norm.

Withdrawal from sexual encounters and interactions are often due to the desire to avoid the issue of sex in their lives. As clients recall their abuse history, the probable feelings of anger, disgust and sense of betrayal concerning the invasion of "intimate space" and uninvited contact during the experience(s), can precipitate a conscious distancing from sex encounters.

Sexual orientation and/or identity confusion issues are often surmised to be impacted by experiences of sexual abuse or incest. It makes sense that this kind of abuse would influence sexual development in many ways. Maltz and Holman (1987) hypothesize that female survivors represent two different groups: women who are lesbian and who happen to be incest survivors, and women who are basically heterosexual or bisexual and who have experimented with female partners as part of their trauma reactions or healing process. Many male survivors have been abused by a male offender and this inevitably raises questions, and becomes the core issue for the survivor, as he explores his sexual orientation. (Dimock 1988, Hunter 1990) All survivors, regardless of gender, need to explore their sexuality, so they can feel more comfortable about themselves and their sexual preferences. Then they would no longer predicate their sexual decisions based on fear and avoidance, but rather awareness and choice.

An inability to differentiate affection from sex is a common experience for survivors of incest or abuse. Undoubtedly as children, they were expected to give affection to the person who was perpetrating the abuse. It is likely that they sought affection from this person as well. Profound confusion arises when a child receives sexual attention *along* with nurturance and affection, or simply sex without the nurturance. Survivors can confuse affection and sex, and can feel that in giving and receiving sexually, they are getting their needs met and engaging in a fulfilling relationship. This attempt to satisfy much of their emotional needs through sex is likely to leave them feeling empty and wanting. Sometimes this sexualizes the survivor so that she may continue to seek out partners who will finally give her the emotional satisfaction that she craves. Survivors need assistance in coming to a better understanding of the loss and grief (see above) associated with the abuse, as well as the ability to redefine sexuality as a single component of intimacy.

The use of sex as a control mechanism relates to the survivor's belief system regarding the use of their sexuality, allowing her to accept the notion that to gain attention or keep control of relationships, the survivor's most valued asset is sexuality. Power and control, if not available through other means, can be gained through their sexuality. We can assist survivors in acknowledging their positive attributes and values, while their limiting conscious and unconscious beliefs that sex is their only asset is debunked. The survivor can then reclaim their sexuality in positive ways, integrating into a more healthy adult self.

> Samantha was sexually abused by her father regularly during her adolescent years. At sixteen, with the help of her then current boyfriend, she decided to disclose her abuse. Her father was arrested, but never prosecuted, and the "suggestion" that he receive counseling was ignored. For her own safety, Samantha determined that she could not reside in the family. She ran away from home, and married her boyfriend, who raped her on her wedding night, when she refused his overtures to consummate the marriage. She quickly left him, and joined the military, as her way to distance herself from her past.
>
> Samantha entered treatment when her third marriage was deteriorating, and she reported feeling no closeness or connection with anyone in her life. She acknowledged that her incest history played some role in her choice of men, particularly men who offered her no hope of long term commitment or intimacy. She tearfully recalled a period lasting approximately two years, while in the military, she engaged in forty-seven one-night stands. She was able to recount in some detail, every interaction, including names, places and dates of the encounters. During the initial course of treatment, Samantha began to understand the enormous level of emptiness and sadness she felt about her life. She could appreciate how these many unsatisfying sexual relationships represented her attempt to find intimacy and connectedness, hoping to replace what was lost with her father and other significant relationships. As individual and group treatment continued, Samantha examined "distance" of her husband in the present relationship with regard to her inability to feel safe and protected by him. The marriage eventually ended, when she attempted to negotiate changes within the relationship, with which her husband was unable to comply.

After several additional failed attempts at establishing positive relationships with men, Samantha finally found "Mr. Right." They are happily married, and have one child. The issue of childrearing, and the parallel fear of duplicating her own abusive childhood, previously had prevented her from being able to see herself as a capable competent parent.

SELF-DESTRUCTIVE BEHAVIORS

As discussed above, feelings of guilt, shame, blame, and anger are often difficult for the survivor of incest to come to terms with in an adaptive way. Because of their negative feelings about themselves that were fostered in their childhood abusive experiences, many survivors engage in self destructive behaviors. The motivations behind of each survivor's self destructive behaviors vary quite markedly. All involve some measure of self-directed hatred and rage often operating at an unconscious level. These behaviors can be conceptualized along a continuum from less to more severe, and there can be overlap between them. Survivors have explained that their self destructive behaviors were a way to block out or mute their emotional pain; an expression of self-blame and hatred of the body; a way of converting deep-seated emotional pain into more manageable physical pain; as a way to exercise control; as an 'expression of anger or as a way to block out feelings. There are a number of ways to express self-destructive behavior: self-mutilation, eating disorders, sexual acting-out, chemical dependency/addictions or substance abuse, and, in its most significant form, suicidal ideations or actions. These are discussed below.

SELF-MUTILATION

One of my clients said, *"I can always hide away from people how I really feel about what my brothers and uncle did to me, but, at least with these long scars on my arms, people somehow know that I'm hurting."* Self-injury is a survival skill. For some, it is a replication of the actual abuse. Clients have related that by hurting themselves, they have the ability to repeat an act of abuse, but this time they are controlling the injury and the degree of pain they experience. This seems to be comforting. The survivors report that they get to stop the pain whenever they want to. Their pain has an end, and this time, *they* are the ones who are in control of it.

Some survivors injure themselves as a way of releasing some of the pain they feel on the inside. Their inner world is full of torment and unbearable suffering, but it doesn't show on the outside. No one knows how badly they feel. Hurting themselves is a way of making the pain visible. Cutting or mutilating becomes a cry for help; it speaks for the survivor.

Many survivors experience relief when they are hurting themselves. It relieves some of the internal "pressure." The physical pain hurts less than the emotional pain, and therefore it becomes a welcome distraction from intense anguish the survivor feels on the inside. They may be so numb, that they need the intense physical stimulation of self-mutilation to have *any* feeling at all. Making themselves bleed is life-affirming to them. It proves they are human and alive.

Self-mutilation can also be precipitated by anger and self-hatred turned inward. Cutting themselves may be the only "safe" way the survivor knows to express anger. Survivors also cut themselves when they feel scared or believe they "deserve to be punished," particularly when they make some type of breakthrough in their recovery.

The more a survivor gets in touch with their emotions and their anger, and learns to express them in more appropriate ways, the less compelled they will be to hurt themselves.

EATING DISORDERS

A wide range of eating disorders has been associated with abuse, from overeating to the extent of obesity to the opposite extreme of bulimia and anorexia. Anorexia has been explained by a number of survivors as a way of feeling in control of themselves, and also a way of displacing anxiety about the abuse in to a more manageable form of anxiety about body shape.

Bulimia has been described by sufferers as a way of purging guilt or expressing self-hatred. Some survivors overeat, using food as a source of comfort. Others deliberately try to gain weight in the hope that they will become less attractive to others, and thus become safer from sexual advances. In most cases, the incest survivor does not overcome these disorders until the underlying cause, the incest, is treated. If an eating disorder is present or suspected, it should be treated concomitantly with the incest issues. (Dolan 1991)

CHEMICAL DEPENDENCY/ADDICTIONS

The correlation between chemical (alcohol and drugs) dependency and incest has been noted repeatedly. Survivors begin using/abusing alcohol and drugs after the trauma in order to relieve stress and to self-medicate, a way to forget, to feel good, to be "their real self," or simply to numb the pain, or block their feelings entirely. When a patient who is chemically dependent presents for treatment, the incest issues become secondary to the immediate issues of the client achieving and maintaining sobriety. Sometimes sorting through the maze of problems related to abuse of alcohol or chemicals obscures the issue of the abuse which may have generated it. Obviously this presents a problem for determining an appropriate diagnosis and treatment plan. Clients who are actively abusing chemicals or substance are not good candidates for incest-focused therapy until they develop healthier emotional coping strategies. Clients should be encouraged to enter into a detoxification program if necessary, or at the minimum begin an active participation in a twelve step recovery program. Many therapists will not begin incest-focused therapy until a client has six months of sobriety or drug-free time. Clients should be cautioned that as they progress in their sobriety and the prior suppression benefits of "self-medicating" wear away, they will in all likelihood experience more intense symptoms related to their incest. These symptoms then can more appropriately become the focal point of the treatment process.

SUICIDE

Therapists working with sexual abuse survivors need to recognize that they are more likely than other clients to present both suicidal ideations and a history of past attempts. Numerous research studies have clearly indicated the significant relationship between a history of incest and suicidal behavior.

Briere and Runtz (1986) found that the incidences of suicide among child incest victims were twice that of children that had not been abused. Suicidal ideations and thoughts are frequently related to the negative self-perceptions, particularly self-blame, shame and guilt that survivors feels. Suicidal gestures and attempts can be interpreted as a "cry for help" by the survivor, especially when the real or perceived message given to them, both during and after the incest has stopped, has been that the abuse can not be openly discussed.

A seventeen year old, Bert, was brought in for counseling by his mother because he had taken his father's shotgun into the woods nearby, and left a note saying he did not want to 'be around anymore.' During the second session, Bert admitted that he had been molested over a period of several years by a mentally retarded uncle who had come to live with them. The bind of wanting it to end, not wanting to hurt his grandparents by accusing one of their children of this abuse, having doubts about his own sexual identity, and being absolutely petrified to develop a close relationship with his girlfriend was torturing him. He could see no alternatives. Bert was very angry at his parents, the world and particularly at himself. He could not envision that he had any redeeming qualities. His cynicism was overwhelming and intense. I (Jill) acknowledged the particular pain that having this bind could cause, and reframed his cynicism as a protective mechanism to prevent his ever getting hurt again by someone he trusted. His note and retreat into the woods was a cry for help that his parents could not ignore. I complimented him on how well it worked. We discussed the concepts of PTSD and its symptoms that we could normalize; he was able to physically feel a sense of relief. Since the uncle had died in recent years, I reassured him that he did not have to inform his grandparents who were elderly and very ill. While we were dismantling the bind, Bert had only to come to terms with his own trust issues and healing.

We began to discuss the qualities that Bert liked in other people. As soon as I took the therapeutic spotlight off of him, the answers came easily. We compiled an extensive if not exhaustive list. He was then to take the list and check off those qualities and adjectives that he thought his best friends would describe him as being, since people are usually attracted to others who have similar values and qualities. Finally, I asked him to pick those qualities he would admit to having for himself. For the first time, I noticed a slight smile and the therapeutic work proceeded from there.

When a client is threatening suicide, we do not always have the luxury of time to discuss and deal effectively with the underlying causes for the client's feelings. Before therapy can deal with these issues, the immediacy of the risk of suicide must be addressed. This may require the therapist to take a more active assertive role in the assessment process. While we try to co-operate with our clients and empower them to find ways to take care of themselves, this may be insufficient to prevent a risk of suicide. The therapist needs to be much more directive in conveying to the client that we are not going to let them hurt themselves. Although things at this particular time may seem out of their control, and the only way they believe that they can regain control of the situation is through suicide, these clients must understand that these feelings can pass with time, and that collaboratively the therapist and client can generate alternatives to this behavior.

A tool both of us use with clients who have expressed suicidal ideations or thoughts is a formal written "contract." When I (Mark) developed this contract, I attempted to make it broad enough to cover deliberate attempts, as well as actions that were more impulsive and careless ("accidental"), so as to let the client know that I view gestures and threats seriously. The wording reads:

CLIENT-PATIENT SUICIDALITY CONTRACT

I, _____, contract with Mark Hirschfeld LCSW-C, that I will not in any way knowingly or unknowingly harm myself.

In the event that I am experiencing any desire or feelings to harm myself, I agree that I will notify Mark Hirschfeld LCSW-C, immediately. If Mark Hirschfeld LCSW-C is not available I agree that I will contact another supportive contact with whom this contract has been discussed, and who previously has agreed to offer their assistance.

In the event that neither option is available, I contract that I will immediately contact the local emergency department at the nearest hospital. I will notify them of my involvement in treatment with Mark Hirschfeld LCSW-C, and once my condition has been evaluated, I will have them make all necessary efforts to contact him as soon as possible.

Signed: _____

Witnessed: _____

Date: _____

After the contract is signed, *both the client and therapist keep a copy*. It is important to remember that contracts for the prevention of suicide do not offer total security and assurance that a client will not harm herself. However, it demonstrates to the client that we are concerned enough about their well being to reinforce the significance and importance that we give to that client safety within the therapy process.

DISSOCIATION

Dissociation symptoms can be a coping and defense mechanism for victims of childhood sexual abuse. It often occurs when there is an intense dichotomy between the actuality of the abuse and the world stage on which our clients must play their roles. The secrets become a vise which tightens painfully as the inability to leave or to discuss the situation is made more evident as the victim grows older.

Gloria, at age 40, came in to discuss her unhappiness with her career. She had been under a great deal of pressure from her family to get into a field which was "fitting" and which would provide her with an income, so she dutifully became a secretary. Gloria hated it and wanted to pursue a career in singing. She had always enjoyed singing in the church choir, but recently had been unable to "sing out." She was the daughter of a evangelical minister, who preached in a church where she, her mother, and younger sister were expected to be in the front row being models for the congregation. Habitually, two or three times a week, he would crawl into bed with her and molest her, telling her it was God's will that he teach her about loving. His sermons were filled with passion and retribution for sinners. Although she did not fully understand "hypocrisy" at the time, Gloria knew something was very wrong. Believing that she was protecting her younger sister from this experience Gloria dutifully told no one.

Her relief was that she allowed herself to float up to the ceiling where she could "sleep." She developed a very angry, protective energy which trusted no one, and a very small, helpless, terrified "little one" who had neither strategy nor resources to help herself. Her mother was passive and weak, and spent her life literally pacifying the father to prevent his temper from flaring. In designing our work together, I (Jill) focused on allying with each ego state sequentially, and allowing each to express emotions and psychological needs, as well as to feel understood, appreciated and validated. She recognized that she did the best she could when she was a little girl and literally had to do whatever it took to survive. Gloria also realized that as an adult, she was aware of her personal strength and community resources and could do many things differently if he ever threatened her again. We painstakingly constructed an internal "executive" part who could reassure and nurture not only the "helpless" little person, but to nurture, love and reassure the very angry energy she had stored inside. As therapy progressed, Gloria discovered her "voice," and began singing at first personally, and later progressed to a professional level.

In conclusion, the emergence of these themes will vary from one survivor to another, depending on how potent these negative belief systems are for the individual, but most, if not all, of these themes will surface at some point in the survivor's trauma resolution, and require attention during the therapy process. By their nature and impact on the survivor, these intrinsic beliefs necessitate attention and exploration in order to facilitate positive long term resolution. The methodologies and strategies of intervening therapeutically are investigated in the following chapter.

[3]

The Power of the Therapeutic Alliance

Contrasting Ericksonian and Solution-Focused Techniques and the Traditional Approaches in the Treatment of Abuse and Incest

> Each person is a unique individual. Hence, psychotherapy should be formulated to meet the uniqueness of the individual's needs, rather than tailoring the person to fit the Procrustean bed of hypothetical theory of human behavior.
>
> Milton H. Erickson, M.D.

Over the course of the years that we have focused on the treatment and recovery of incest and sexual abuse survivors, we have found there are many myths and fallacies surrounding the more traditional treatment approaches used as well as the inordinate amount of time credited with being necessary to produce effective change. These fallacies can deter us from inquiring about or discussing incidents of sexual abuse with clients. The prevalent belief that effective treatment is a long-term, overwhelming ordeal is often endorsed by our colleagues and cited in much of the literature. In contrast, solution-focused approaches focus on the concept that therapy is not meant to be forever, nor does it have to be painful or overwhelming. We can better understand the validity of the philosophical concepts that form the framework of solution-focused psychotherapy by stating some of the most common myths and refuting them.

Some of these myths and fallacies are:

"Survivors of incest must emotionally relive and re-experience the trauma in order to effectively resolve it."

This, in itself, may well discourage many from seeking relief from the post-traumatic stress which is so common among survivors. The traditional model of working with clients who have been abused could be called the "un-experienced experience model." This model promotes the idea that people who go through a trauma dissociate from their emotions, sensations, perceptions or other experiences during that time. This lack of connection to the events in turn would lead to the array of present symptoms. By this reasoning, if the problem lies in the past, the therapist must help the client regress into that traumatic time so they can remember, re-experience, and relive the intense emotions which had been repressed, or at least denied. A commonly held assumption is, *"For you to properly heal, it will have to get worse before it gets better."*

The reality is that survivors have only to acknowledge that it happened to them. Going through intense abreactions is *not* necessary, and may slow recovery, as if they had to scrape open whatever healing of the wounds have enabled them to get on with their lives. It is in no way necessary for the client to relive the pain. The emphasis is on allowing the client a forum to tell her story, which can be acknowledged and valued.

"Everyone who has ever experienced childhood abuse is psychologically, emotionally or sexually damaged by their experiences. If they do not know they are damaged, they are in denial or possibly dissociating."

In fact, some survivors are often extremely well adjusted and have become strong adults, determined to maintain their personal integrity and prevent such abuse from ever happening again.

"Treatment of incest victims must be long term otherwise it will minimize or deny the significance of the trauma or the post traumatic effects."

Short term therapies are often desirable in that they offer clients hope that effective change and recovery will not take *another* lifetime to accomplish. Because short term therapies present solutions and healthy alternatives, clients begin to feel better more quickly. Insight can be more effective when one can look *back* on the pain in the past, rather than looking *forward* to 'going through it again.'

"Children never lie or distort perceptions."

Research verifies that memory does not become well organized or vivified until around the age of four. Clients may be simply remembering pieces of parts of their life that they need to organize in their mind in a way that makes sense. It is not an exact replication of the moment. It is simply a piecing together of bits of memory in some coherent way. The fact is that some young clients do indeed distort facts sometimes because they are influenced by an upset parent wanting to find a way of punishing a former estranged partner or spouse. They may have found a way of getting attention and sympathy, or perhaps because they are angry with an adult, and are savvy enough to know what will generate the most trouble.

"Adult memories of abuse are always accurate."

This is the heart of the 'false memory syndrome' controversy. Memory is a 'freeze frame' of moments of one's perceptual reality. It is often a confabulation of events as traditionally demonstrated by having a group of people witnessing a staged event and when asked, gives widely different accounts of what happened. A less naïve point of view is that some adults may be motivated to make accusations to find a convenient scapegoat for their present problems or to detract from personal responsibility for taking appropriate charge of their life. Ironically, therapists sometimes contribute to the confusion by assuming that *any* presenting problem is the result of incest or sexual abuse whether it is a relationship problem, weight problem, drinking problem, etc. The therapist may use the possibility of early abuse as a convenient explanation. Because we have degrees and certificates on the wall, this explanation takes on greater significance, and our client may buy into it.

"Clients who were victimized as children never had a choice about or were accountable for their actions in their abuse situations."

This is one of the hardest notions for therapists to accept and to consider sharing with their clients. The idea of accountability in no way means that it was *their fault*. It certainly does not mean that they seduced the perpetrator, whatever the relationship. It simply stresses "What did I do in that situation? What, if anything, could I have done differently?" What are the reactions following the abuse experiences that belonged to them?

Clients need to address their accountability in the sense of acknowledging their actions in those experiences. The concept of "accountability" serves several purposes. The first is to help our clients view the entire experience more objectively. They tend to place themselves in the spotlight of responsibility. This allows them to openly explore the whole concept of responsibility so they understand and appreciate that they may not have had enough power to change the events. It can also generate observations about how their responses would be different in the present, "knowing what they know now."

The most important message you can give your clients is the permission to put those events into the past and to keep themselves firmly and safely anchored in the present. To accomplish this, we might say something like: *"When you were three or five or seven years old, you did the best you could with what was available to you. It is important for you, as an adult, to understand what you did in that circumstance. It doesn't mean that you were wrong or to blame in any way."* We want to educate our clients about the fact that if they were as young as eight, ten or twelve years old, they may have experienced a pleasurable physiological response to the sexual abuse. Unnecessary guilt often results because the experience felt good. They have to understand that our bodies are specifically designed by nature, so that sensual stimulation feels good. It insures the continuation of our species. Survivors can appreciate that just because it physically may have felt good, doesn't mean that it was a good thing to happen to them.

MILTON H. ERICKSON, MD

At the very core of our collaborative approach to help survivors heal from sexual abuse is the philosophy and approach of Milton H. Erickson, MD (1901–1980). Often regarded as the father of modern clinical hypnosis, Dr. Erickson's career was focused on clinical work, writing and teaching. His success in treating difficult cases in unique ways as well as allowing others to study his therapeutic approaches provides us a model for helping abuse survivors in effective ways.

Dr. Erickson was a psychologist as well as a psychiatrist who promoted the use of clinical hypnosis to help his patients find resources inside themselves to solve any problem that they encountered. One can expound for many chapters on "Ericksonian Principles of Psychotherapy," and this has been done by many other authors. Suffice it to say that his 'utilization concept' which maintains that a therapist should start where the client is, and utilize everything that occurs in order to build and accentuate personal internal resources is at the heart of the Ericksonian approach. This is not only respectful of the client, but effective in establishing the necessary rapport which generates trust and comfort. Matching the client's body posture, significant gestures, voice tone, linguistic syntax and expressions allow the client to feel that at an intuitive level, you can understand and reflect back what they might be experiencing. Is the client using expressions which indicate that she is cognitive, or talking from their logical, rational center of being, or at a 'heartfelt" or gut level which is dictated by their kinesthetic or physiological center of being illustrated by 'organ language' such as "I don't have my 'heart' in this," or "I can't 'stomach' the man." Expressions and language patterns that a client uses can be matched by the therapist in order to construct solutions which will be the most influential in helping the client make appropriate changes. While minimum attention is given to the problem and its origin, the maximum attention is given to the exceptions and solutions. The idea of psycho-pathology is strongly de-emphasized. The idea that just because they have been abused doesn't mean it affects and predicts everything that goes on. The abuse is *not* the only cause of their life problems, and certainly doesn't prevent people from acquiring skills, developing personal assets and resources and coping styles.

> Erickson appears to approach each patient with an expectation that change is not only possible but *inevitable*. There is a sureness which exudes from him, although he can be unsure if he wishes and an attitude of confidence as if it would surprise him if change did not occur. (Haley, 1967a, p. 535 *emphasis added*)

The 'Ericksonian' therapist assumes that every person has all the internal resources and healing mechanisms that they need. The unconscious mind is seen as a creative and beneficial resource, a storehouse of knowledge and experiences. The therapist's job is to merely help guide this healing mechanism to mobilize itself.

We want to encourage a client to appreciate that she has specific and wonderful resources inside that are available to help solve problems in many ways. One "Ericksonian" metaphor has been very helpful in demonstrating these terrific competencies to our clients.

We point out that she has been able to successfully engage in activities of competence from the time she was very young. The explicit descriptive phrases, adapted from Dr. Erickson, proceed along the following lines:

> You learned that you could take a hand and purposefully move it to your mouth which is the basis for feeding yourself. Learning to crawl is the basis of balance from which you learn to walk, and then to run. A teacher introduces twenty-six strange looking symbols, which you soon learn are the letters of the alphabet. You can distinguish an M from an N, a B and a D, and additionally learned the twenty six lower case letters that transform into words to which we impart meaning. Then when these letters changed to cursive, you had to do it all over again.

This adaptation of what Ericksonian therapists call a 'learning set' to demonstrate to a client that they have a history of mastering complex information and skills, implicitly demonstrating that they have the internal resources and inherent abilities to do all the work necessary to heal.

Another concept that Dr. Erickson espoused is to add flexibility and creativity to our approach to both the client and potential solutions. The "right" approach is the one that works for each individual person. Metaphors and analogies reminiscent of the client's experiences as well as strategies which suggest solutions can be introduced to bypass her natural resistance to change. Once our clients can believe that they have the ability to do whatever they need to do, that they can begin to imagine and create the possibility of succeeding.

In the traditional therapeutic model, survivors are often viewed as having been "damaged by abuse." In the "Possibility" or Solution-Focused Model, the client and the therapist both are seen as having an area of expertise. While the therapist possesses the training, skills and potential techniques to help someone develop new strategies and mindsets, the abuse survivor is viewed as having all the internal strengths and abilities that she needs, and the abuse history may influence though does not determine either the present situation or the future. Healing is perceived as a collaborative effort rather than the having the therapist project himself as the "expert." The goals of therapy are individualized with each client. The idea that clients are regarded as *"unique individuals"* mandates the belief that the treatment for that individual and her problems is equally unique. It is dictated by the client's presentation rather than the therapist's perception of what the client needs. Being creative, flexible and observant in our approach to initiating the therapy process, we can make it more fun for ourselves as well as being even more effective. Depending on theoretical orientation and discipline, we frequently get caught up in what we learned in graduate school about how the therapy is *supposed* to be conducted, instead of allowing the process of treatment to evolve. As one of my colleagues once said "One of the worst things we can do as therapists is to come down with that awful disease, 'the hardening of the categories.'" This relates to the idea that you have to conduct therapy a certain way, with a certain approach to be "right." If the actual process doesn't fit or work the way we thought it would, what then? We have to avoid complacency and ritualistic ways of thinking. If something is not working, do something different; and if it is working, do it some more.

> Our primary and ultimate loyalty as clinicians must be to our patients and their needs, not to our colleagues and their theories.
>
> Alan Gurman (source unknown)

These strategies, and the messages embedded in them, concern the power of individuals to engage in a different course of behavior and action. These behaviors are viewed as being in their best interest, and presently their best choice. Our belief system about how people empower themselves to acknowledge, value and validate their life choices, is one that forms the basis for the theoretical framework of how we work with our clients. It supports the ideal concept of collaborative healing, which gives our clients an awareness of how life experiences and choices affect them, and how, with therapeutic support, these choices can be examined. This collaboration empowers our clients to determine whether or not these choices continue to be in their best interest.

Ultimately as the situations and circumstances involving these behaviors are explored, clients are helped to become aware that those choices they made were the best available to them at that particular moment in time. These abuse survivors can then "forgive themselves" for some of their past behaviors that they currently identify as unacceptable, while empowering them to come up with new responses for similar experiences. The idea that behaviors that worked in the past may no longer be appropriate, and thus new responses to situations can be developed. This can include reactiveness to stimuli that previously caused abreactions or flashbacks. The work of Erickson, Satir and Berne create the template for change that allow for the healing to occur.

NEURO-LINGUISTIC PROGRAMMING

Neuro-Linguistic Programming or "NLP" is a behavioral model and a set of explicit skills and techniques developed by John Grinder and Richard Bandler in 1975. Defined as "the study of the structure of subjective experience," NLP studies the patterns or "programming" created by the interaction between the brain ("neuro"), language ("linguistic"), and the physical body, that produces both effective and ineffective behavior in different contexts. The skills and techniques that are encompassed by NLP were derived by "modeling" or precisely explaining the patterns of excellence that effective therapists such as Dr. Erickson, Virginia Satir, Eric Berne and others used in the course of treating their clients effectively. Once a model or template for each intervention is developed, we can teach our clients the strategies and skills derived from that model.

The effectiveness and efficiency of NLP to help people change are derived from certain assumptions, or what the NLP community refers to as 'presuppositions' which underlie all the therapeutic techniques and strategies and provide appropriate frames of reference about one's ability to change that have been very powerful in helping our clients make healing changes. Although this is not an exhaustive list of the presuppositions, we have selected those which seemed to be the most salient in our treatment strategies and adapted some presuppositions to use as guidelines for working with abuse survivors.

People interpret the world from their own internal maps rather than from sensory data.

This means that everyone has personal filters created by their experiences and belief systems. We must meet the clients at their model of the world. This might mean mentally stepping into the situation as the clients have described it. This increases rapport with the client and avoids judgmental opinions or comments.

Clients make the best choice for themselves at any given moment based on events, skills and experience.

Human beings tend to seek out pleasure and avoid pain. They do not try to make their lives difficult on purpose. They formulate their actions and reactions based on their prior experiences, knowledge and expectations. To the extent that our clients can acknowledge and forgive any errors in judgment, they may be able to redirect their future actions towards a more positive outcome.

Respect all messages from your clients, whether verbal or non-verbal.

Each has value and importance to the client. We focus on expression, gestures, tonality, or even silences as meaningful responses which are congruent or incongruent. This does not mean that we confront, challenge or draw attention to any incongruent responses. We merely note them and find an appropriate time to inquire with a sense of curiosity about possibilities.

Meet clients at their model of the world.

This allows the establishment of true rapport and an unconditional acceptance which leads to trust, and ultimately opens the client up to the possibility of healing and changing behaviors, responses and emotions.

Anything that happens in one part of the system affects all parts.

A systemic, holistic approach recognizes that every being is an interactive organism which also interacts in the environment with other persons, and events. It is important to remain curious and inquire about how making even desired changes might affect or impact other aspects or relationships in our client's personal, physical and/or emotional environment.

Teach choice; never attempt to take choice away.

If a belief exists that one has no choice or only has a choice between two options, then we truly put ourselves on the horns of a dilemma. There are always more choices, alternatives and options which can be created. We never want to take choice away—even negative ones. We want to add relevant choices and the flexibility to use them as we might find appropriate to the context and situation.

Experience has structure; if you change the structure, the experience must change.

When anyone engages in a particular behavior, she frequently does so based on previous experiences, consciously or unconsciously. One replays what happened before, and determines whether a repeat performance is helpful or disadvantageous. If she determines that a different course of action is required or necessary, and changes the structure of the experience even subtly, the possible outcome will likely be different. The examples can be found in some of the common rituals that we engage in. Every day, for months on end, you drive to work using the same route with the same traffic jams, with the same frustrations and stress. Today, you find the route totally blocked and you are forced to take a detour. You may find that there are fewer traffic lights, wider streets and less traffic. You are empowered to shift your perceptions of reality, thus allowing you to have a choice. You may also immediately understand that there are always options and you have the ability to do or accomplish the same objective in a better way.

If you always do what you've always done, you'll always get what you've always gotten.

If what you have been doing doesn't work, you have to do something different. Rita Mae Brown of Alcoholics Anonymous and the twelve-step program is fond of saying: *"Insanity is the act of doing the same thing over and over and expecting different results."*

While traditional therapy is 'past' oriented, solution-focused or 'possibility' therapy is connected to the present and the future. To the extent that the experiences of abuse have influenced the present, and are expected to affect life in the future, our clients can be empowered to make appropriate changes. The abuse must be relegated to the distant past from where it can be objectively and safely viewed, rather than relived. "Change involves a process of initiating (and promoting) observed *new* and *different* behaviors and/or perceptions (frames) within the context of the presenting problem (and the patterns of behavior which surround it) and/or the solution for the problem." (deShazer & Molnar, 1984)

Clients need tools and techniques that will allow them to access unconscious resources and project themselves into the *future* that is successful, with better understanding of their history, and with a more perceptive belief that they are doing better. The concept of the "miracle question" was developed by Steve deShazer (1988) and is one that solution-focused psychotherapy espouses as especially valuable. It is especially valuable in keeping clients oriented to what they want for themselves rather than staying stuck in the victim's role. This question was modified by Yvonne Dolan (1991, p. 34) to specifically address issues relevant to the treatment of survivors of abuse, and asks:

> If a miracle happened in the middle of the night, and you had overcome the effects of your childhood abuse to the extent that you no longer needed therapy and felt quite satisfied with your daily life, what would be the first thing you would notice that would alert you that a miracle had occurred and that things were different?

It is not a rhetorical question. It provides a glimpse of how our clients might see their future when therapy is over and things are better. We need to allow our clients to spend some time formulating an answer, even if they struggle to see the future, or plead ignorance of a positive response. This is grist for the mill of therapy. We can encourage them to create an answer even if it doesn't make much sense to them. They have permission to create or invent several thoughts, ideas or even fantasies about these possibilities. The rationale is that if energy, creativity and thought are focused on and invested in alternative behaviors and futures, these will begin to manifest as reality.

As the client begins to formulate these perceived futures, we need to make sure that the responses are *possible* outcomes. It is important to help clients avoid frustration by understanding that their need to "fix" things from the past involves events that are unchangeable. Help them focus on the do-able, the possible or changeable, all those aspects of life that are within their control.

"The focus on *actions* moves the discussion into the realm in which the person has some choices and power to make changes." (O'Hanlon, 1998 p.89) In looking at the clients' solutions for the future, we can help them realize that people evaluate themselves and their life choices in large part based on how others see them. Therefore a component of the Miracle Question is built on the reactions even a small difference will make to those others involved in the client's life. The predicted responses of others help the client to change their own expectations, and thus change their behaviors and feelings. Once a client has a strong internal conceptualization of success, such as life with more acceptance of their history by themselves and others, they can spontaneously do something different, so that this vision of the future can be a reality. The client is empowered to dissociate from the negative events and associate into the possibility of a solution. These therapeutic tools give our clients strategies and options with which to effectively manage contemporary stress.

Accessing a state of comfort, security and/or competence is an important asset in healing from abuse or incest. The three options consist of: accessing calm or competence experiences from the clients own personal history, guided imagery in which the therapist creates an experience of calm and/or competence in the session, or modeling the competent, resourceful behavior of someone whom the client admires.

The methods of accessing these internal resources are adapted directly from NLP frameworks. We have included specific "how-to" templates for these interventions in Appendix A. The first is a model for *"Creating a Personal State of Calm/Competence"* in which we help the client recall moments of time that they have experienced calm or competence. I (Jill) often give clients assignments at the end of our first session together to remember at least three times in their life in any context when they experienced "calm, relaxation, safety, peace or security." I want to help them define the experiences as pure states, those which are not tainted by negative emotion. An example is that she might remember a safe experience cuddling with her grandmother in a big rocking chair. The next thought relates to the fact that Grandmother died two months ago. Although the initial memory is a wonderful resource, the fact that the emotion of security is mixed with one of sadness makes this memory less effective. I might make the suggestion that she think of a 'sliver of time' when she felt calm and secure. We can then expand that 'sliver' hypnotically, so it seems like all the time in the world. For each of the three, she is then encouraged to associate into that experience: " . . . seeing what she sees, hearing what she hears, and feeling the internal sensations that she experiences." We can now use hypnotic language patterns to reinforce and intensify the selected memory. The second is termed *"Externally Oriented Self-Hypnosis."* This technique was originated by Stephen Gilligan, and modified by Yvonne Dolan from whom I (Mark) learned it. It allows the client to have an experience of comfort and security, have access to unconscious resources, and maintain an external focus of awareness. We stay connected to the present by allowing the client to keep her eyes open, create a present, stable context and maintain demonstrable security while in a hypnotic state. This increases her sense of control and makes flashbacks or anxiety much less likely.

The third strategy for achieving resourceful states is modeling another person's behavior or internal state. The concept is that when one imagines what it is like to be inside another person's positive experiences, they have to access a similar experience inside themselves. Even though they are attributing these emotions to another, in fact, they are the only ones experiencing thoughts, images and sensations.

These internal resources are used to separate the client from a feeling of helplessness or hopelessness in encountering memories of the abuse. I (Mark) have the survivors begin to write down the memories of their experiences, keeping a five-day journal. This allows them to translate events into words focusing on the mastery of their life which feels so out of control. Writing dissipates negative emotions and the structuring of the narrative serves as an ego-enhancing experience. When clients complain, *"I can't write. I don't know what to write, or I can't remember anything."* I invite them to, *"Take this magic pad and this magic pen and put them beside your bed every night."* Carla came back with seven and a half, single-spaced (front and back) pages recounting the events in explicit details, down to the color of her argyle socks, what her father did to her and that it happened to her when she was fourteen. I ask all my clients to write, to journal for five days at their own pace and at their own speed. Thus it is not an unending assignment, nor is it overwhelming in scope. Their writing is theirs to keep or to share, as they deem appropriate. The appropriate timing may be months or years after. Georgette, another client that I (Mark) saw a number of years ago recently mailed me a package. She wrote, *"I thought you might want to see this."* The dates on the pages were from 1984 and 1987. *"Now I am ready for you to see what I wrote."*

Some of the best methods to relieve Post-Traumatic Stress Symptoms in the Ericksonian tradition were designed by the originators of Neuro-Linguistic Programming, Richard Bandler and John Grinder, who modeled Dr. Erickson, and described how to replicate Dr. Erickson's apparent therapeutic wizardry. For many years, the 'Visual-Kinesthetic Dissociation Technique," created by Richard Bandler and John Grinder, (1985) in their book, *"Using Your Brain—For a Change"* has been effectively used to diminish the intense aftereffects of the abuse. The basic frame of reference underlying this intervention is that it is important for the client to be immersed in a state of safety and security. We then help her maintain a double dissociation from "movie screen" images of the traumatic events. This better allows an objective, unemotional perspective which relieves the intrusiveness of the memories. Once the "movie" of the experience has played out at a "fast forward" speed, the survivor can nurture and validate her "younger self" who has survived that trauma. This is effective even if there are multiple incidents of trauma and sexual abuse. An adaptation of this treatment pattern that we have found helpful to use is included in Appendix A.

Pearl is married with two young children. Over the years she had tried to ignore the fact that she had been sexually molested by her father because she had been encouraged by her mother and brother to "put it behind her" to preserve family unity. The stress of having to put up a front had begun to affect her relationship with her husband and children in terms of explosive anger when she believed she was not in control of a situation. She finally recognized the connection of the abuse with her relationship problems and sought counseling for resolution of the problems. After I (Jill) had helped Pearl access her personal states of safety and competence, we reviewed the process so she would cognitively know what to expect. The next session, Pearl practiced the elements of the process individually before we put them together. We began by imagining that her cognitive faculties would be in a projection booth in this "theater of the mind," from which she would objectively view the movie of the "younger self" experiencing the traumatic events on a small screen far in front of her. When it was over, she imagined she could step inside the movie screen and comfort, validate and nurture the younger child that she used to be. When the process was over, Pearl announced that a heavy weight had been lifted from her shoulders and chest. She was astonished that it had been so easy to do and she could feel such a remarkable difference. She was excited about learning more strategies to resolve the remaining issues.

Over the years, clients have asked me (Jill) about how they could have survived the trauma of their abuse without either visiting this abuse on their own children or feeling embittered and cynical. As we talked about the events in their life, it became clear that they had been validated in their fears, their anger and their grief by others who were close to them, sometimes without the other's specific awareness that they were having that impact.

Emily shared that a very warm, empathic social studies teacher in high school, had broached the general subject of sexual abuse perpetrated by adults, and gave a specific pronouncement to the entire class that *"the victim is <u>never</u> at fault, even when the perpetrator tries to pass on responsibility, guilt or embarrassment to the victim. There is never an excuse that justifies improper touch, invasion of personal propriety and assault."* Emily reported she felt so empowered by this revelation that she sat down with her mother that night, and informed her mother that the stepfather had been molesting her for over a year. Completely shocked, her mother insisted that the step-father move out immediately, until she could determine exactly what happened. Over the subsequent weeks and months, her mother was able to piece together the entire story. Emily had felt believed, vindicated and whole when her mother initiated both criminal charges and divorce proceedings. Emily was very comfortable talking to her mother who listened sympathetically and empathically. Bolstered by this empathy and counseling, Emily felt prepared for the intense emotional experience of a trial which incarcerated the perpetrator for a long time. As a result, Emily did not integrate or come away with any feelings of insecurity or guilt.

Some clients are besieged by intrusive flashbacks. It is as if they are experiencing the events all over again. There is a certain irony that these flashbacks seem to occur out of the blue in a climate of relative safety and security. Sometimes they occur in the office itself. While you can reframe the meaning of them as an indication that the survivor is emotionally strong enough to face these memories—and deal with them differently, these flashbacks are very upsetting to those clients who want to be in control of their emotions, and by implication, their lives. Sometimes, therapists themselves are unprepared for these intense emotional experiences that appear without warning. There is nothing more taxing to a clinician than seeing a vulnerable client sitting on the floor, rocking back and forth in the fetal position. That it can occur in the relative comfort of your office and in your presence may represent the fact that you have effectively established the necessary trust and safety that allows these memories to be expressed and shared. As professionals, we are in the best position to make an important impact on these post-traumatic symptoms. Our therapeutic power is derived from the fact that we are objective observers as opposed to being "stuck" inside the "larger than life, continual loop" experience that seems to have no ending that our clients endure. The treatment strategy at this point is to first validate the experience with a verbal recognition of what is happening in the present. This separates the events of the past from the reality of what is occurring now. Speaking firmly and confidently, you can validate the experience by saying: *"You are having a flashback! We are going to focus on some strategies to deal with this experience now."* This statement identifies the symptoms as a process which can be understood and remedied. Grounding the client in the present by reminding them of the security anchor, asking them the day and time, asking them to tell you about what they see at this moment in the office. Ask them to touch something in the room which connects them with the 'here and now.' We want to help them evaluate this experience in its entirety; the onset and the ending, the negative and the positive, the sensory aspects and the cognitions with the objectivity of an adult perspective. We chunk down the experience, disrupting the gestalt. Adult cognitions and objectivity gives clients the ability to conceptualize what a flashback is.

One of the assumptions of the Ericksonian and NLP model is that *"Experience has structure. Change the structure and the experience must change."* The structure encompasses the qualities of the components of the gestalt or the perceived experience. The experience of this negative memory is separated into the visual, the auditory, and the internal physical sensations which can include olfactory and gustatory elements. This allows the client to make specific, purposeful changes in these qualities, even in minute degrees, resulting in distinct shifts in how she experiences the memory.

Joanne complained about panic attacks which were triggered by intrusive memories of incest experiences. As we discussed ways of treating the problem, we focused on changing the internal images of the experience which seemed to trigger the negative internal sensations. Joanne spent at least one entire therapy session accessing and integrating internal resources of security and comfort. She understood that these would serve to diminish the effects of the traumatic images which she imagined were projected in front of her. She described the relevant qualities of the images of the abuse as if she were describing a photograph or a painting to a friend over the phone. Shifting the specific visual qualities of these images had an effect on the intensity of the internal responses which had triggered the panic. For example, the sounds which accompanied those memories even became muffled, indistinct, and significantly diminished in their power to terrorize her. Joanne reported that she began to feel more comfortable. Washing out the color in the picture to more resemble a pen and ink drawing reduced the intensity even further. Joanne began to smile, saying it looked more like a cartoon. The final shift occurred when she imagined that she could view the entire image as very small, making the image look even smaller as if it were the size of a postage stamp against the far wall. Joanne practiced this 4–5 times, each time making the changes faster. The disturbing memory was depotentiated and the panic attacks diminished in both frequency and intensity. She believed she had put the incest in the past, and felt very much in control of her life in the present.

In conclusion, we believe it is important to encourage our clients increase their internal comfort levels so they can move forward with their lives. We have included our favorite methods of intervening effectively to change the intensity of the experience for our clients. Over the years, I (Mark) have used a simple acronym that was introduced to me during one of my myriad training experiences which I have found to be helpful in remembering the elements needed to protect our clients from re-traumatization as they begin the healing process. It is termed: **"S-E-L-F"**

S —**Safety** and therapeutic bonding established between therapist and client. The *"Structure"* of treatment includes appropriate therapeutic boundaries and the parameters of intimacy. *"Self-care"* appraises any health or medical issues, compulsions or addictions and stress management. *"Support systems"* focus on the "external world functioning" such as the home environment, amount and kind of exercise and recreation, the degree and impact of dysfunctional relationships.

E —**Exploration** of memories of the abuse from the present, safe state. This includes the aftereffects of the abuse, such as: bonding with the perpetrator, possible fear of family reactions, or ego splitting, *Examining* any threatening childhood messages, memories and cognitive distortions in the light of adult experience and logic and normalizing reported symptoms.

L —**Loss** and grieving which involves self-compassion, (rather than self-pity), an understanding what was lost (trust, innocence, family and friends), mourning the changes, acknowledging betrayal, expressing expected concerns about forgiving, seeking repair of the damage and/or appropriate compensation.

F —**Fulfillment** relates to an integration of the new learning, reconnecting appropriately with her physical body, using emotions as signals that she needs self-care and love, renegotiating important relationships, validating her sexual identity as well as acknowledging the importance of humor in life. Clients can use symbolic tasks and/or objects to help externalize the problem and to make concrete transitions from the past.

[4]

A Therapeutic Model for Working with Survivors

> The goal of abuse recovery treatment is not to remember or substantiate trauma per se. It is to learn to live congruently, presently and functionally with the facts of one's life. Ultimately, the work is not as much about what others did to one as it is about how one's early experiences still ricochet in mind, emotion and body and what one may do about this in the present.
>
> Caloff (1994)

A road-map is helpful to keep us driving on the appropriate streets and highways to reach those new or unfamiliar destinations where we have never journeyed before. Similarly, formulating a therapeutic guide or philosophical "road-map" for working with the abuse survivor population will help us stay on the main thoroughfares or at least suggest interesting and effective detours or side streets when those more familiar roads are obstructed or rendered ineffective by the uniqueness of our clients. This chapter attempts to suggest one such model. To be sure, it is not the only one which is effective. Hopefully, it will present a secure starting point from which creativity and diversity can spring.

Every survivor of incest or sexual abuse has her own story to tell, and her own journey to take. There is no generic recovery process that works for all survivors. To work effectively with survivors, we must develop a flexible ever-changing "reference map of recovery." This map is a collaborative working plan or "construct" that we intuitively develop as we begin working with a client and get a sense of her own strengths and resources. The therapist and client will use this plan as a guide throughout the treatment. The "map" should utilize only the most "adequate and acceptable" means (techniques) to support that specific individual client's understanding and adjustment and recovery of their incest/sexual abuse. After getting their history and perception concerning their experiences of sexual abuse, it is the therapist's responsibility to learn how to "read and follow this map" in order to provide the most appropriate treatment approaches and techniques to facilitate change for the client. These techniques can reflect the different theoretical frames that a therapist has encountered as they evolve in their training, experience and philosophy. However, they must be responsive to the client's needs and feelings.

The healing process for sexual abuse survivors is designed to allow those survivors to stop feeling contaminated and defined by their abuse experiences, thus the trauma ceases to influence their thoughts and/or behavior patterns. In turn, we expect that our clients will allow their inner feelings and thoughts to come into conscious awareness with respect and appreciation which enables clear, purposeful choices rather than being controlled by the unconscious, maladaptive behavior patterns instilled inside as a result of the abuse. In short, they begin to take control of their lives.

Survivors need to learn to trust themselves and their perceptions, and be willing to take appropriate risks in expressing and exploring their current world and their role in it. Treatment can help the survivor to heal the psychic injuries and wounds caused by their abuse.

Healing sexual abuse wounds is a dynamic process of evolving cycles whereby the survivor is always moving along a time continuum. Sometimes she may focus backward in time to the traumatic material; at other times, lurch forward into anxiety about the present issues with which she must cope, and to those real fears of an unknown future. We can provide a sense of safety and comfort by emphasizing their competence and security in the present. With each cycle they acquire additional resources to deal appropriately with both the traumatic memories and their impact on the present. The clients move through the therapeutic experience with an internal support system strong enough to reclaim those "parts" of their identity that were lost or damaged by the abuse. Successful therapy also may mean that some clients have experienced their first respectful, and non-exploitative, interpersonal relationship in their lives.

To begin the healing process, it is imperative for the survivors be prepared for what is ahead as they embark on the healing journey. Initially, they may be extremely concerned or even anxious about the therapeutic process. For some, this is due to previous negative therapy experiences. For others, therapy is venturing into unknown territory. They simply do not know what to expect from the therapy experience, including the fear of possible consequences of exploring their past (and previously undisclosed) abuses. These fears can be partially allayed as both the therapist and client discuss the process of healing. Having a familiar format for therapy makes it easier to orient clients to what they can expect. This should include a discussion of the client's motivation, prospective outcomes and expectations of therapy. We should also be direct and honest with the client, and make clear that the healing process is not always an easy one. There may be appropriate times during the therapy that she will be in as much (or even more) discomfort and pain as she had experienced at the beginning of our work together. Helping her access and anchor positive internal resources of calmness, safety and security will help cope with these moments of difficulty.

Jay Haley, the renowned family therapist, believes,

> The purpose of therapy should be to help the patient in the most adequate, available and acceptable fashion. In rendering aid, there should be full respect for and utilization of whatever the patient presents. Emphasis should be placed more on what the patient does in the present and will do in the future more than a mere understanding of why some long-past event occurred. The sine qua non of psychotherapy should be the present and future adjustment of the patient (Haley, J. 1987)

We need to have an expanding repertoire of skills available to formulate specific treatment strategies for each client. An individualized concept of how the therapy process progresses, including appropriate goal setting, naturally occurring phases of life, necessary tasks or emotional stages facilitates the integration of the "recovery map" and the successful treatment outcome for the client.

Briere (1987) stated that therapy should be "portable," meaning that the client should be able to take certain skills and coping strategies away from each therapy session that they can use in their daily living. Therapy with survivors of abuse, perhaps more than with any other therapeutic population, always should include a significant educational component. This is especially important in those cases where the client has not been severely traumatized by the abuse, or when there are time constraints due to insurance (managed care) mandates, or even within an inpatient setting where the client is available daily for two weeks or more. Since many survivors believe that their experiences were unique and that they were singled out to be abused, by providing information about other people who have been abused, our client may possibly feel less isolated. Providing information concerning the dynamics and impact of sexual abuse helps de-stigmatize the situation and helps clients to see that their reactions and responses were normal rather than pathological. When it is integrated with specific skill building and coping strategies, the opportunity to experience qualitative change in emotions and behavior is enhanced.

To facilitate this healing, the survivor often needs to go back and re-experience those aspects of their childhood that have been long "forgotten." This process of the healing involves reclaiming some of the lost memories and experiences, both positive and negative, of their life or "picking up some of the pieces left behind." For many of the clients we see, the trauma, pain and the "hypnotic tapes of childhood" forced the child aspect of themselves to retreat inward. As adults, they are afraid to retrieve those lost memories for fear of re-experiencing the emotions and physical sensations associated with the abusive experience. Therefore, they may disavow any knowledge or conscious awareness of childhood. These "forgotten memories" are important to reclaim as they allow access to important memories, experiences, and resources that to this point in their lives have not been available. Once the survivor believes that she is safe, and in touch with current reality, she can be reassured that the memories of the negative experiences will be acknowledged, validated, and valued—without risk of being judged. With the assistance of a nurturing supportive therapist, the client's pain (of childhood) can be recognized and released. The client is then freed from using those limiting survival strategies adopted from childhood in the present and future. When recognizing the fact that her "child" part has survived the traumas and mistreatment, she can open the door to the possibility of developing "self-loving" rather than self-hating perceptions.

With time, the client is invited to accept responsibility for "reparenting" the parts of herself that were inadequately parented in her childhood, reassured that the therapist is available to act as a guide or coach in the process so that she has sufficient support for the task. (Crowder, 1995) She can incorporate all the resources and utilizing all the lessons learned through those negative experiences so they would never be repeated. Thus, the adult ego state is charged with the responsibility to protect a vulnerable, less resourceful 'inner child" part from any further violence.

We refer to the "inner child" as that aspect or part of the survivor who holds these memories and feelings for the adult client, and getting in touch with this internal repository is an important part of the healing process. The positive aspects of working with the inner child allow the survivor to break through old, outdated, dissociative defenses which enable the expression of feelings and memories. As clients begin to see their "child" part as having survived being traumatized and mistreated, they can open the door to the possibility of developing "self-loving" rather than "self-hating" perceptions. This allows a sense of innocence and playfulness to be reclaimed.

For many survivors, the inner child metaphor is difficult to accept initially. Being childlike or having childish ways of reacting to situations is seen in a negative light. It is often helpful to reframe this childlike quality and ability to enjoy life experiences as a positive sign of healing. Some specific dialogs and techniques relevant to working with the "Inner Child" are discussed further in Chapter Seven.

A MODEL FOR WORKING WITH SURVIVORS

To formulate a therapy process that is educational, portable and manageable to the client, and able to be integrated with both short and longer-term interventions, the treatment of survivors of incest must accomplish specific goals which can be viewed in six phases, each with sub-sequences. While each phase will be addressed separately more completely in the following chapters, the following is a brief summary of the working model:

I. Forming a Therapeutic Alliance
Forming the therapeutic alliance encourages the client to begin acknowledging, talking about and exploring the feelings associated with the incest experience. This alliance is an essential part of the successful therapeutic experience. This needs to progress slowly and deliberately. To assist this process, we need to explain the parameters of therapy to reassure those clients who may be frightened by previous negative experiences or confused and apprehensive about what to expect in therapy. It is our responsibility to decrease the client's anxiety and establish a firm beginning level of comfort and

safety. We want to create an environment that will enable our client to trust us with their stories.

Most of the people we work with are women, although some male survivors do come in for treatment. Statistics demonstrate that one in four women have been sexually abused before the age of eighteen. They also show that one in every seven men have been abused by this same age. Because gender is a significant issue when dealing with a survivor population, this issue is raised immediately with my new patients. I (Mark) do this because it is a way of showing empathy for what's possibly going on in their life. It is not unusual for women who have been abused to view all men as at least prospective perpetrators. Particularly when the presenting issue is the lack of significant interpersonal relationships with the opposite sex, I want my clients to know that I realize that they may have some concerns as to whether or not I might become a perpetrator as well. Acutely aware of the way I interact with my clients, I want to make certain that there is neither an assumption of "inappropriate intent" on the part of the client nor any verbal or nonverbal indications that I will become an abuser or perpetrator. I openly discuss with women clients the possible concerns they may have working with a male therapist. I explore their prior relationships, and general feelings regarding men, and try to assure them that I will not exploit the confidence they placed in me by coming to treatment.

II. Challenging the Belief Systems

It is important to address the belief systems and/or embedded messages that our clients have internalized as a result of the abuse they have experienced. These unconscious rules or "scripts" are negative or limiting internal beliefs that are focused on psychological impasses. These include feelings of *helplessness, hopelessness* or *worthlessness* that the clients may experience as they attempt to navigate the choppy waters of life's challenges. These belief systems translate into habitual and automatic responses that exist outside of a client's conscious awareness. They tend to feel limited, but they are not quite sure why or how this occurs. One way we can tell that a belief system is at work is that our client reports she "cannot remember a time when she did not feel rejected or incompetent." A limiting belief crosses time and situational boundaries to continue to infect the present. We talk to clients about having and expressing feelings, yet the challenge becomes to help them to understand with accuracy what their feelings are. If a client says "I feel depressed," how does she differentiate it from an experience of sadness or one of gloom? What does 'happy' or 'excited' feel like? All these different kinesthetic sensations that define how we distinguish various emotions occur at different places in the body.

An important concept for trauma victims to identify is the difference between having an emotional response and feeling a physical sensation. This understanding of normal physical reactivity and "feeling a feeling" is a significant breakthrough for the client especially when dealing with issues of sensuality and sexuality. The personal confusion that could have begun with the "pleasant sensation," which was initiated by inappropriate sexual contact as a child can now be examined with greater clarity. We can help our client to differentiate the now understandable physical reaction from the appropriate negative emotional response to unwanted or unacceptable touch. As clients continue their recovery and even attempt new relationships that may allow intimacy, they can be freer to understand what emotions they are feeling and to respond appropriately. We can also teach them specific strategies to access personal resources of safety, comfort and security, if the emotions don't coincide with the physical sensations they may be experiencing.

The most optimal treatment course is to challenge the belief systems of a client's past, as she gains new insights about the family dynamics surrounding the incest and the impact on the child then as well as the adult's coping and surviving skills.

III. Integrating the Functional Adult with the "Inner Child"

Integrating the functional adult with the child is the mechanism that allows the survivor to nurture and acknowledge her victimized inner child, which encourages the development of continued positive self-esteem that leads to a sense of empowerment and self-worth, and as well as improved physical and mental health.

Through integration, all aspects of the survivor's personality can be explored and affirmed, whether operating in the adult self or in the child ego state. Many survivors have found that through the integration process they have learned not only to love and honor their "inner child" but also to reclaim their childhood. Thus many are finally able to the experience child-like joy and pleasure they were denied and deprived of in their actual childhoods. This reclamation is necessary for healthy adult functioning.

This is also the phase of treatment that enables a client to establish or reclaim a positive identification with her body. This identification encourages positive feelings of sensuality and sexuality, as well as the ability to have functional, healthy, and personally meaningful relationships. Accomplishing this allows the client to begin to experience reparative relationships with significant adults that reflects, models, and teaches about caring relationships with well-defined boundaries.

A positive image of self allows clients to be more aware and responsive to "gut" reactions to experiences which previously had been minimized and ignored. As self-abusive clients reclaim this connection between self and her body, it helps stop cutting or other mutilating behaviors.

Probably the most meaningful reaction to empowering a survivor to (re)establish feelings about her body is the new found or rediscovered joy of everyday sensuality, an awakening of the feelings that may have remained dormant since childhood.

IV. Confrontation and Disclosure

Confrontation and disclosure are very powerful therapeutic tools which foster growth and healing. While they have substantial benefits for some survivors, they do have the potential for being emotionally damaging and destructive for others.

In this phase of treatment, the client would give themselves permission to disclose the abuse or incest to family or others and/or to confront the abuser(s). It is important for the client to first consult with the therapist to mutually determine if the recovery process has progressed sufficiently to undertake this endeavor. McFarland and Korbin (1983) recommended that the motivation of all involved including the therapist be examined in deciding whether to pursue a confrontation. Therapists must understand their own internal motivation for suggesting that a client confront their past to insure against countertransference. The therapist's orientation and personal belief should never determine whether a confrontation is going to occur. Rather the survivor's motivation and goals are the critical factors.

V. Termination of Therapy

As the client continues their recovery and growth, preparing for their future, the issue of termination of therapy arises. The survivor should be given many weeks (if possible) with which to process the meaning of leaving therapy, as feelings of loss may be intense. (Simonds, 1995)

During the termination of the therapy phase, the appropriate care is taken by the therapist to empower the client to move on with her life, with an increased and growing awareness of the respective strengths and assets.

These treatment phases, together with some of the therapeutic strategies that have proved most useful for each of them, are discussed with greater detail in the following chapters.

[5]

Forging the Therapeutic Alliance

Psychotherapy is one of the most taxing endeavors known to mankind. There is nothing that compares to confronting human misery hour after hour, and bearing the responsibility for easing that misery using one's mind and mouth. At its best, it is tremendously uplifting. As you watch the patient open up, breathe. Let go of the pain. At its worst, its like surfing in a cesspool, struggling for balance while being slapped with wave after putrid wave.

—J. Kellerman

Our first contact with any client requires that we establish rapport and trust which improves the success of planning and achieving therapeutic and life-enhancing goals. Working with survivors of sexual abuse means that we need to be even more conscious of the specific vulnerability that this client population may present. This seems to be more significant at the beginning stage of therapy, sometimes even before the actual therapy begins. When survivors start treatment, many do not immediately disclose their abuse history, for a multitude of reasons. These might include fears of rejection, not being believed, or judging, whether consciously or not, that the therapy relationship might not be safe. When we develop an awareness of a possible rationale for client nondisclosure and discomfort, we can understand even more clearly the importance of the initial contact. Frequently, this can serve as a barometer for the eventual success of treatment. This chapter will address the special sensitivities and accommodations that can facilitate a client's smoother transition into therapy. Many of these same considerations are applicable with clients who do not have an abuse history, but who may need a treatment plan which is less intrusive and threatening.

A relevant issue, significant to the ultimate success of the therapy, is the communication process that develops between therapist and client even before the actual "talk" therapy session begins.

We can pay attention to how both verbal and non-verbal communications, and even subtle cues, contribute to rapport and trust. Instinctively, when a client initially telephones for an interview, through conversation, the competent, caring therapist attempts to elicit a connective bond that allows the client to feel comfortable enough to come into the office for the initial interview. It is widely acknowledged that many of our clients, who come into therapy with a history of incest, *do not disclose* this history immediately. Either during the initial telephone consultation, or during the beginning phase of treatment, their presenting problem frequently involves other issues and agendas.

Each person has their own style of interacting with clients. The following are suggestions for you to consider as you think about how you set up the initial contacts with your clients:

When a client arrives at the office, and is sitting in the waiting room, the first thing we tend to do when we introduce ourselves is to stick out our right hand, elbows straight; fingers extended, and say, *"Hello, my name is . . ."* When we extend our hand in that manner, the possible meta-message we are giving to the client is "It's an order! SHAKE MY HAND!" You (as the client) really don't have a *choice*. As a societal norm, when someone extends their hand, we feel obligated to return the gesture and shake their hand. It is the rarity when a person feels confident enough to refrain from extending their hand, and simply exchange greetings. How do we know what the significance of the handshake is to our client? How do we know whether or not a handshake had previous negative connotations and attributes for this specific person? This seemingly innocuous gesture may trigger intense feelings of discomfort as a response to an action by the therapist; and therapy hasn't even begun yet. (or has it?) After all, first impressions will set the rapport stage on which the therapeutic relationship is founded. If we can find neutral ways to introduce ourselves, we may be taking fewer risks. It is important to note that for the vast majority of our clients, this idea of a "neutral" introduction will be unnecessary. When we extend our hand for an introduction, most clients may simply reciprocate, feeling no discomfort. She may even offer her hand first. There is no problem there! However, in most cases, we do not have a great deal of information about the real issues or history of the client. We can never be certain, and it might not be worth the risk when there are other acceptable options available to welcome our clients and make them feel at home. We can simply open our hands as a welcoming gesture and verbally introduce ourselves. If a client offers her hand, we are certainly free to accept it. With this more neutral gesture, there is no obligatory responsibility on the part of the client to "do it or else." This certainly demonstrates respect for our clients and makes no assumptions about them.

It is a forgone conclusion by most clients that we will *not* be using the waiting room to do clinical work. As there may be more than one clinical office in a suite, it seems most natural and appropriate to invite the client to follow along into the office we will be using by either gesturing the direction with a hand, or by saying *"Won't you come in?"* or *"Please come with me."* We may not have given much thought to securing the client's comfort in proceeding into a strange office space. We need to closely observe the gestures, posture or any other non-verbal signals that our client may be experiencing distress or an unwillingness to proceed into the office. It may be that the anticipated confines of a "therapy room" are so intimidating that their discomfort level rises precipitously. If we think outside the proverbial box, we can even do good preliminary work in the waiting room to make sure we have proper rapport. Those therapists who have worked with adolescents can probably relate to doing "7-11," or "WAWA" therapy (name your own convenience store) because the client was more comfortable in those environs. This unconventional means of connecting with the client on a non-verbal or unconscious level may be necessary to communicate that you can be amenable and flexible to unique needs. Since *most* clients will have no difficulty with the more traditional rituals of "following" directions to enter the therapy room, it is important for the competent professional to be on high alert for the ones whose reactions are different.

As the scene shifts to your space where the therapy proper occurs, we may point to a chair, and invite our client to "Have a seat." Once again we need to be alert to signs that our client is reticent to follow our invitation. Where else could they sit? If not on a chair, is it permissible for the client to sit on the floor, on a cushion, not sit at all, and possibly pace the floor. One incident I (Mark) remember fondly is the time I asked a client to "sit anywhere you'd like." So, where did she sit, but in *my chair!* I was okay with that, and made no mention of it. It was interesting that, instinctively, the following week, the client found another comfortable place to sit. I would hope that we could all be flexible enough to tolerate that preference, and make sure that the rest of the therapy hour would proceed smoothly.

There have been times when a client becomes silent in our session, or does not seem to feel comfortable expressing herself, I (Jill) invite her to stand up and walk around my office or even outside in order to interrupt the non-responsive pattern which has developed. When we give the client flexibility and choice, we metaphorically empower her to take control of her life. If we give a non-specific invitation such as *"Please make yourself comfortable,"* we can communicate the clear message to the client that she has choices in therapy and in life, and we respect her ability to make them. Based on our personal therapy experiences, we may remember how it feels to be in a situation where someone other than ourselves seems to have created the "rules." You may want to point out where the rest-rooms are, and offer them any refreshment if you have a coffee maker or water cooler.

Taking a psycho-social history can be another potential source of discomfort for a new client. Often she is not quite sure who in the world you are, whether or not you can be trusted, and may have no idea of what to expect from this initial encounter with you. If you knew *everything* about them, would you think badly of them? Are there legal implications of information they share with you? This is particularly relevant in this age of the new HIPAA rules regarding the disclosure of our privacy policies.

After the necessary details such as name, address, phone numbers, etc. which the clients can fill out while in the waiting room, we generally get around to asking about where they grew up, both past and present family connections, possible medications, etc. As a matter of course, inquiring about a history of abuse is included in the middle of all of the other standard questions. All different forms of potential abuse, such as physical, emotional, verbal, sexual, or harsh punishments are covered in the question. By asking this question face to face, you can watch facial expression, changes in posture, coloration, pauses, or tonal qualities for an indication of abuse in this client's history. A neutral or unemotional response; or a matter-of-fact denial would be congruent with an absence of abuse. Pauses, flushing, making a request to explain what you mean by "abuse" or a response in the positive, even if it is qualified or minimized, are an indication that you may need to gently follow up. Stay in a state of curiosity, using a "Lieutenant Columbo" mindset. One very powerful invitation and permission you can give each client, is to *"Tell me everything you feel I need to know, in order for you to know that I understand your situation."* As they begin to tell you their story, you can acknowledge their experience and validate their feelings about the abuse. You may come to discover that abuse did happen, even though the client was unwilling to share it at an initial meeting. Conversely, just because there is abuse in the historical past, it may not be relevant to the specific issues they have presented to you for change. Nonetheless, having this information is important for your understanding of the total person. These initial series of interactions is where the therapy begins. We forget this axiom at our peril.

ISSUES OF TOUCH

The feelings of vulnerability that many clients feel in the beginning stages of treatment seem to be manifested in the inability to trust people and to feel safe. Fearing that being close to someone can result in being hurt again, clients can be ambivalent regarding the issue of touch. Although some survivors express a need for affectionate physical contact, they may feel frightened if this contact actually occurs without invitation or permission. This consideration is especially important if the abuse generated disassociation from their body and feelings as a defense mechanism.

As competent clinicians, particularly when there may be a history of abuse or incest, we are both aware and respectful of how vulnerable that client might be feeling. There are times a client may request a hug or some type of physical contact, or we may deem it appropriate to ask permission to initiate such an action.

Touching clients is always a loaded issue that raises many concerns. We need to be aware of how each of us might feel about the permission to touch clients under *any* circumstances. If we can explore our own views of touch and its multiple meanings, we can effectively handle this issue with a client. Some liability insurance policies specifically prohibit any kind of therapy that requires physical contact with the client. If the clinician is uneasy with any physical contact for any reason, he or she must express this to the client and eliminate it as a therapeutic possibility. In the recent environment of increasingly litigious interactions, many therapists are afraid to initiate any type of touch for fear that it will be misinterpreted or seen as non-therapeutic. Uninvited touching may even result in a vulnerable and needy client instigating some type of malpractice action.

A colleague reported one experience he had (before the advent of managed care) when after two years of successful therapy with a female client, she had come into the session proudly declaring that she had completed her doctoral dissertation. Without a second thought, the male therapist reached out to shake her hand to offer congratulations. The client was offended by this seemingly benign action, which adversely affected the therapeutic process for a considerable period. If that seems bizarre, we can remember that their experiences may have been bizarre enough to make logical interpretation of "normal" actions abnormal.

Even if a clinician is comfortable with the notion of therapeutically appropriate touch, it remains imperative that he ask the permission of the client for the act of hugging, or touching in any way. Touch can express a message of caring, empathy and comfort to a client when done appropriately. It can also be reminiscent of the seduction of the abuser to the client. Through a therapeutic discussion, a client can learn to conceptualize the difference between a positive, nurturing, appropriate physical connection and an exploitative, sexual touch. We can further assist the client in learning about healthy boundaries and limit setting. Limits and boundaries that are consistent, and neither overly permeable nor rigid, can be established on behavioral and/or cognitive levels.

Most sexual abuse survivors have experienced touch as sexual or unsafe, so that a therapist should practice prudence in enacting and maintaining a collaborative touch contract. It is imperative to obtain permission from a client before initiating even the most limited type of touch. Even if our client is in a deeply regressed or abreactive state, we must first have that "touch contract" before attempting to "orient the person in the present."

Asking permission communicates respect for the person, body and entire being of our client. It states that her concerns or preferences will be heard and respected. One of my (Jill) clients mentioned that she was unnerved and annoyed because a former male therapist insisted on sitting too close to her. She wanted to keep anyone at a distance so she could see where his hands were and be able to move if necessary. *Any* touch should be by permission and only along the lines of a pat on the shoulder or a grasp of the hand. Alternatively, we can use a verbal cue which can equally well anchor the client into the here and now, such as calling out her name, or even using a cue

word that our client agrees will connect her with her own competence and control. There are always options.

There are moments in the therapy process when a safe
touching experience can be a healthy and healing experience for the
client. You can set up a physical anchor for safety and security that
you both agree on, such as the client asking for, or reaching for *your*
hand. When immersed in the recollection of painful experiences, she
may possibly feel abandoned and alone, we can extend a hand and
offer comfort and safety during this intense moment. While holding
this link to reality, she may more easily move through and past the
traumatic thoughts and feelings. When an abreaction occurs, an
abuse survivor may be crying as she recounts a particularly painful
element of her experience or loss. We may want to offer a tissue,
acknowledging the client's need to cry and shed tears, while validating her right to have and express the feelings. There are times, especially during or after a difficult session, when she may specifically
ask the therapist for a hug. Survivors have experienced betrayal in
most significant relationships; therefore they may initiate physical
or sexualized contact to test a therapist's trustworthiness and his
ability to maintain boundaries, and a safe therapeutic environment.
This is when you might choose to offer both your hands for her to
hold as a mechanism of additional comfort unless a specific "contract" is made to do otherwise.

Whenever we work with survivors, it is imperative to maintain
and evaluate all boundaries and limits, as well as to establish dialogue with our clients about the meanings of their behavior. If both
the *therapist* and the *client* understand the meaning of a touch, and
have specifically "contracted" and agreed to the context and meaning in which it occurs, then physical contact (i.e. a hug) can increase
the sense of client safety.

There are many therapeutic options, which do not involve any
touch, that provide a sense of security and safety for clients. We can
use symbolic tasks and objects to represent safety, security and the
present time frame for the clients.

Invite the client to walk around the room and find a space or
object in the room that represents comfort or safety. The client can
get a physical sense of the space and as they walk around it, they can
get a metaphorical awareness of ownership and safety. We can place
a chair in that space where the client can sit; or invite them to hold
the object if they need an "anchor" which represents security. One
way that I (Jill) use seating as a security anchor is to *invite* my client
to sit in *my* chair and look at the problem from that perspective.

Many clients report that they actually feel more balanced and competent as they imagine that they see the problem through my eyes. A client can adopt internal imagery or cue words that are associated with a state of safety and security to provide nurturing. A symbol or object of faith can be a wonderful resource for encouraging internal strength and determination. One of my clients, Jean, discovered that she could finger the cross she always wore around her neck, and connect with that feeling of security and peace that she found in church. She was able to make peace inside herself and relieve her sense of misplaced guilt and self-revulsion.

These are the poignant human moments in the therapy when the therapist can become a caring adult, responding as if the person were not a client. As Roth (1993) states, within the context of a trusting relationship with well-defined and well-maintained boundaries, the client will experience these occasions as very special. However, the therapist must maintain extra humility in making such decisions, for it is well-documented that some misguided therapists have used a rationalization that having sex with clients is "therapeutically helpful." Sadly, there are therapists who may even believe this. In fact, like the abuser, they are only using the clients to satisfy their own needs.

FURTHERING THE ALLIANCE

As we create an environment to encourage therapeutic connections with our clients we do so in order to increase the comfort that clients can feel while telling their stories. The process of treatment involves encouraging them to begin to talk about exploring and acknowledging the feelings associated with the abuse experience. Clients need to have their experiences/feelings acknowledged particularly if they do not remember the abuse, or are uncertain that it happened. The concept of acknowledging is not the same as believing the abuse or being able to prove it in a court. Clinicians are not legal investigators. We leave that to the forensic experts.

In the model of solution-oriented treatment of sexual abuse, the three core concepts are *acknowledgment, valuing,* and *validation.* We acknowledge people by letting them know that we have noted their experiences, points of view and actions. It is important to reinforce the value of our clients as unique, competent human beings. The guilt or regret often results in believing they are less valued. We can validate the reality of their perceptions helping them recognize when their actions and/or responses are appropriate and relevant in the context of these experiences.

When we look at solution-focused work, there is a supposition that the primary focus which brings many of our clients into treatment does not include their abuse experiences. We focus initially on the complaint that brought the client into our offices. Then we determine what is not working or what is bothering them in their current life.

We can't assume that every client needs to go back in time and "work through" the memories. Some will and some won't. EVERY-ONE IS AN EXCEPTION! It's important to keep focused on the goals of treatment rather than getting lost in the gory details of the problematic past. Focusing on the past keeps the client enmeshed in the problem state without perspective on how to solve their issues. Sometimes clients have been convinced by books, other therapists, media stories, or just the current fashionable "conventional wisdom" that they must remember details about the abuse in order to resolve their current problem. You can acknowledge this view and gently offer another—that focusing on the current issue can be a way of resolving and possibly even remembering the details in a safe, secure environment.

CRISIS PRIORITIZATION

To protect our clients and ourselves, we must ascertain to the best of our ability that no sexual abuse or exploitation is currently occurring. If discovery indicates that it is, our work together must emphasize the immediate need to secure our clients safety, report this abuse to the appropriate authorities and marshal the necessary resources to stop it. No previous sexual abuse material should be explored in great detail if the survivor indicates that she is in the throes of another personal crisis. We must defer to this current emergency, and help the client with a more directive approach in order to get her back on track by giving her a specific direction and a goal to accomplish. It is crucial to *prevent and avoid* the precipitation of a new crisis, the exacerbation of the present situation, and/or the promotion of regression and decompensation. *Crisis intervention comes first.* Although necessary, this prioritizing may be tricky because some problems are not responsive to treatment until their functions and secondary gains are uncovered.

Martha had been in counseling for about three months. We had been making some progress with regard to the after-effects of her abusive childhood. She was very intimidated by men in any authoritative role such as supervisors where she worked, and responded poorly to evaluations or even constructive criticism. It still came as a shock to her when she was "laid off." Whatever self-confidence she had been building came to an abrupt end. She was particularly concerned that her husband would desert her if they were dependent only on his modest income, since their relationship was very shaky (in no small part, due to her past abuse).

The first thing we did was to have her update her resume. I (Jill) reframed this apparent setback as an opportunity to find a new work environment. I related her layoff to the economic reality of this particular company rather than to a personal rejection. There were additional employees who also lost their jobs. The second recommendation was to seek out an employer or work situation with women managers. She also mentioned that she might be happier working in a small office environment. She was assigned the task of going to the local Chamber of Commerce to investigate the size, management structure and personnel of different local companies. It took another three months for Martha to get all her information together, do her research, get the appropriate forms in to the selected companies, set up the interviews and to continue to think positively about herself through it all. She finally found a job which she thought she could enjoy. She also investigated her opportunities to become self-employed to make some extra money in case her husband did leave.

Although her husband continued to blame her for losing her job, he did not leave her. A strategy for getting him to change his hostility was initiated by telling him that the only way she could be successful in any new job was to have his confidence and support. Although he did not verbally agree with her, she reported that the incidences of hostility and accusation definitely decreased in intensity and frequency.

Regardless of what we discover from our client's history, we do not give any messages that they are "damaged goods" or that their future is determined by having been abused *in the past*. Remember that change can occur in the interpretations of the actions/interactions associated with a particular series of events. As we listen to their stories, it may become necessary to make provisions (contracts) for safety from suicide, homicide or other potentially dangerous situations.

We want to use whatever strengths, resources and/or survival skills that our clients have developed over the years, possibly as a result of having survived the very abuse which has been haunting the client.

What are the natural abilities that our client has developed in spite of the abuse? Clients are encouraged to focus on positive abilities or qualities they developed as a result of the abuse, as well as any effective coping mechanisms they have evolved in efforts to deal rationally with the abuse. Perhaps they have been surprised by the competent or innovative way they have dealt with something stressful or how they have stopped themselves from acting on destructive impulses. When we focus on these more positive frames-of-reference, we help clients value themselves and widen their life perspective so they recognize there is more to them than the abuse. By gently challenging evidence of self-blame, shame or demeaning narratives they may have accepted from others in their lives, they can transform and reframe negative identity stories into positive victories. This helps re-organize their thoughts about the future to generate positive behavior patterns.

Once an abuse survivor can acknowledge, validate and value themselves, she can concentrate on developing achievable goals which will only further enhance motivation, enthusiasm and self-esteem. A sample of the kind of solution-focused questions that we use to generate forward-thinking positive outcome questions is included in Appendix C.

When the client focuses on these positive, goal-oriented questions and the appropriate answers, there is an implication and a presupposition that she will initiate different, relevant behavioral responses which will change her life.

Many clients maintain there is often a little voice of self-doubt, neediness or self- degradation that invades their daily life encouraging risky sexual behavior. It puts a man's perceived needs at a higher value than protecting integrity such as: *"You're not really that important. You need to do whatever is necessary to keep him."* All efforts to shut this voice up seem to be ineffective.

The following exercise is one of the most effective methods of accessing personal validation, marshalling positive unconscious resources and creating a future orientation of accomplishment and success:

> Imagine that you have grown to be a healthy, wise, old woman—and that you are looking back on this period of your life. What do you think this wonderful, wise you, (who knows you better than anyone else in the world) would suggest to help you get through this current phase of your life? What would she tell you to remember? What would she suggest that would be the most helpful in helping you heal from the past? What would she say to comfort you—and does she have any advice abut how therapy could be most useful and helpful?

> Write a letter to the 'older, wiser self.' Tell her what you are struggling with right now. Allow that 'older, wiser self' to immediately write a letter back giving affirmation, comfort, advice as well as helpful instructions for getting through this period of your life based on her wisdom, years of experience, and objective perspective.

This exercise can also be designed to write this letter to a deceased, but supportive significant other.

These concepts reframe the effects of their experiences, and validate the clients as being *victors* rather than *victims*.

In summary, this chapter has focused on getting the healing process off to a good start by valuing the space, story and sensitivities of our client, particularly at the early stages when we have not had the opportunity to know them well. This reinforces that we are trustworthy, sensitive, caring professionals and will do what we can to collaborate with them to help them heal. It sets the stage for the establishment of mutual trust and respect so that we can tackle the strange new world of identifying their limiting beliefs, challenging and replacing them with more empowering ones. These strategies are presented in the next two chapters.

[6]

Challenging the Limiting Belief Systems

Nothing is as dangerous as an idea, when it is the only one you have.

—Emile Chartier

Events, particularly traumatic ones, often have an impact on the psyche that affects the very core of one's being. Since the majority of our incest and abuse clients have been victimized as young people, they tend to be "imprinted" with these events such that each occurrence begins to define their identity, or *who* they are as people. A belief begins to develop about the world and one's place or role in it. Beliefs are internalized generalizations about the world which create emotional boundaries and "filters" that interpret reality in ways which either limit or empower us. They influence our ambitions and impact the choices we make: *Is the world a safe place in which to live? Can I trust the people with whom I live or have connections? Am I smart enough, good enough, worthwhile enough to dream—and achieve my dreams?*

Distorted beliefs are perceived to be the sources of most mood disturbances, troubled relationships and related problems in adulthood. However, by no means does this preclude other possible contributing factors such as organic causes of depression or self-destructive lifestyles.

The essence of many of the distorted and limiting beliefs of victims is that she perceives herself as having consented to the abuse and therefore holds herself responsible for what happened. Finkelhor (1986) integrates several of the alternative beliefs into the argument that a child is incapable of giving any informed consent to sex. Informed consent requires that the child understands what she is consenting to and that she has the freedom to say yes or no. Apart from their limited understanding of the basic facts of life and sex, children are relatively ignorant and are naïve about what is appropriate sexually within their particular culture. They are equally unaware of the potential damage to their own development and adjustment when they engage in sex with an adult.

Sometimes belief systems conflict with each other or with concrete reality, such that we may deny what is actually happening in the present. Even when an experience of abuse is in the distant past and the abuser cannot be a danger anymore, the insecurity and anxiety still may exist with intensity. Limiting belief systems from our past often prevent us from recognizing or utilizing the resources we have available in the present. If this is true for us, it is even more relevant to survivors of sexual abuse. In transforming beliefs, it is important to remember that even negative, limiting ones can produce positive byproducts which must be recognized, preserved and protected.

> Frances was a 28-year-old who had been molested by her brother with the passive approval of her father. The father had maintained that it was better to "experiment" in the safety of the family, and (wink, wink) "boys will be boys!" The limiting belief that accompanied this abuse and collusion was that she didn't deserve respect and consideration from men. This was manifested in her choice of consecutive boyfriends who continued to show disrespect by infidelity and verbal abuse. The latter was the presenting issue.
>
> Conversely, she had many strengths and resources in other areas. It became very clear was that Frances had become financially independent. She was on the executive track with her company, and had been recognized for her achievements on a national level, not incidentally conferred by men who were in authority, who theoretically had no ulterior motives or agenda. We reframed these positive recognitions and intense career energy as the natural and appropriate reaction and outgrowth of being abused by the males in her family. As a result of her early experiences, Frances had determined that she would never put herself in a dependent relationship with a man. It was important to her to protect this value of independence and energy for high achievement when we made the appropriate changes in the emotional environment.

The three therapeutic goals she had set were to: heal from the experiences of the abuse, change the belief about her worth and self-respect and develop confidence in some new strategies for determining the degree of trustworthiness of men she could consider as potential significant relationships. One of the successful interventions designed to heal her from the abuse was to identify and ally with her highly protective energy inside that attempted to prevent further emotional pain. Once we had established this alliance, we were able to obtain an internal permission from this "part" that could allow Frances to continue to value her achievements and independence while seeking qualities and resources in which she was lacking. She recognized that she could choose to change her limiting belief of worthlessness which depleted her energies and created fear and dependence. Frances became optimistic that she could establish interdependent connections with special people with whom she could feel safe in expressing and responding to appropriate intimacy.

When one has been violated and abused, particularly by someone who has been regarded as trustworthy, there is something inside which is destroyed. It may not be repaired just because the abuse and violations have stopped. While common "neurotic" problems will impact certain aspects of coping with the world, limiting beliefs affect *all* the contexts of life and would seem to have been operating throughout one's life. These are the learned internal messages that our clients carry with them about their very identity, how they are supposed to behave in the world, and how they will cope with events in their lives. The acceptance and integration of these messages which can be considered survival adaptations are necessary to preserve cognitive integrity when a client is powerless to challenge an authority system. When a child is degraded, criticized, physically or sexually assaulted, he or she does not have the sophistication, objectivity or adult perspective to know that the failure lies with the abuser. They internalize the messages and accept it as true, rather than challenging or disputing these messages with rational thought. While having a limiting belief is certainly not a diagnostic criterion of sexual abuse or incest, it is all too often a common result of it.

Glenda, age 35, came to counseling for treatment of her depression. She complained that she never found any pleasure in her job or in her family. While she never receives reprimands at work, she is very sensitive to any criticism. When I asked her how long she had been feeling that way, Glenda began to cry and said she could not remember when she did not feel judged and criticized. Her mother had constantly characterized Glenda as "a loser" for tasks she had not accomplished. Her father, a sales representative who traveled three weeks out of every month, had left the family when she was 8 years old. To help make ends meet, her mother had moved in with a male co-worker with two teenage sons, 14 and 17. Two years later, they were married. Glenda eventually developed a close relationship with the younger stepbrother when the older son moved out. This was the only "support" she experienced in this blended family since the stepfather worked up to 10 hours a day and ignored her and her younger sister when he came home. Glenda physically grew into a woman and her stepbrother's attempts to "comfort" her evolved into an intimate relationship. She was overwhelmed with remorse and guilt. When she told her mother, she was met with disbelief, peppered with accusations of seduction. When she was 18, Glenda used college as an opportunity to get out of the house. After two years, she married a graduating senior who joined the navy. They have two children, seven and nine years old. She reported increasing feelings of anxiety about being physically touched by her husband over the past three years. She distanced herself from him, and the relationship deteriorated into arguments and fights. She had no patience with the antics of her children, and in frustration, would scream at them and spank them. When her husband threatened divorce, Glenda became depressed and sought counseling.

We can begin to suspect the existence of a limiting belief system:

1. When our clients report a continuation of destructive or unproductive behaviors,
2. When clients report that they cannot remember feeling competent or worthwhile in their life.
3. When 'tried and true' mechanisms of accessing internal resources are denied or blocked.

Part of the therapy is to identify specifically what the limiting belief is, and to determine if there is anything about that belief which has value in the present. We can help our clients to look at these messages or internalized beliefs and assess whether or not they have any value to them. We want to preserve positive elements of the belief, hold on to certain ideas or change others, so that we can transform those negative elements of that belief into a resource or an advantage, such as the need to be protected or vigilant. Challenging the limiting belief systems encompasses the changing of the "problem frames of reference" and the ensuing identity stories which defines not only what they believe, but who they *are* in the world as well as the role they play.

Most of these survivors carry with them four basic 'stories' or beliefs which last a lifetime and interject themselves into their lives:

- A sense of *self-blame* for *everything* that happens.
- Invalidates their experiences suggesting that everything that they feel or know about their history or experience is wrong, untrustworthy and cannot be relied on.
- They had and continue to have *no choice* about anything that happens in their life—everything is beyond their control.
- Change is impossible.

We want to help clients create more empowering, positive internal beliefs to replace the outmoded ones which had contributed to survival in the past, but have long since lost their relevance in the present. There are several methods of countering these pervasive beliefs. One way is to linguistically challenge the immediacy of these concepts by speaking about the problem in the past tense: referring to *"That's what <u>had</u> happened back then—<u>now</u> there are different opportunities and circumstances."*

When they complain about the immutability of their situation, it is our opportunity to reframe their negative statements into positive ones. *"So what you really want is to find a relationship that is healthy and beneficial?"* We must assume the prospect that clients will find the solution with the resources that they either possess or will learn. We need to use words such as "yet" or "so far"; words that give them the subtle sense that not only do you, as the therapist, believe that change is possible, but that they are completely competent to achieve positive change. We can chunk down the elements of the desired change to reinforce the idea that they are already engaging in certain aspects of positive behaviors—things they do that are indicative of progress or success which may be unconscious or out of their awareness.

Using the asset of objectivity established by natural maturation, the time which has passed since the origin of the traumatic events, and the anchoring of states of competence and security, clients can successfully challenge their personal sense of shame, guilt, and self-devaluation. Once we shift to a forward looking and goal-directed frame of reference, clients can begin to focus on their resources and capabilities rather than on their perceived limitations. We can validate the fact that they have the right and permission to value their experience, feelings, sensations, thoughts and body. This objective, non-emotional reference reconnects the mental, emotional and physical aspects of the self, facilitates the integration of new learning and resolves any cognitive distortions and defensiveness. Through positive belief systems, we evaluate our capabilities, and construct appropriate strategies to accomplish goals we have set.

The method I (Jill) use to help a client identify these limiting beliefs and develop more empowering beliefs is adapted from the "Re-imprinting" model of Robert Dilts in his book, *Changing Belief Systems with NLP* (1990) The theoretical basis for this therapeutic model lies in the concept that young people can create an 'identity-forming experience' which defines one's self-concept often based on a single experience.

> If a female child has been physically abused by her father, the imprint when she grows up will create an interesting pattern. In spite of what she wants to do, or what she knows logically, she will often get herself into abusive relationships, because that imprint is like an archetype for how the relationship with a man should be.
>
> If a female child has been abused by her mother, when she grows up, she might somehow wind up abusing her own children and hate herself for it, but she won't know why. This means that your early experiences don't only affect your feelings, they create very deep role models for relationships. (Dilts, p. 103)

The goal of re-imprinting is to access the appropriate internal resources which are presently available in the adult client that can 'heal' the internalized abuser, thus transforming the early dysfunctional relationship or dynamic system into a healthy one which can empower positive change. The strategy itself is derived and adapted from the work of Robert Dilts (1990) and is included in Appendix D.

Glenda decided to first re-imprint the relationship with her mother, and then the one with her step-brother. She identified her limiting belief as "Never Good Enough." As she worked through the process, she created a new belief, "I Am Competent and Confident."

The experience with her stepbrother was somewhat more complicated. She recognized he was insecure and irresponsible. She came to recognize that not only did she *deserve* happiness, but she was capable of having it with her family. She and her husband started couples counseling, and they are working on their interpersonal issues which have developed over the years.

One simple mechanism which helps to externalize the problem is to use symbolic tasks and objects to make transitions from the past into the present and onward toward the future. Invite the client to look around the therapy room or office for an object or symbolic space which represents a sense of safety in the present time. We can explain that if the therapeutic work somehow becomes overwhelming, they can focus on this object or symbol or move to that safe space to reconnect with the present so we can talk about what *had* just happened. It is important to shift the language relevant to the trauma or abuse into the past tense, which further dissociates the negative feelings, and 'anchors' them to any symbol they defined as safe. We can encourage our clients to engage in this process of finding symbols of security in their homes as well.

There are two therapeutic interventions that we have found effective to help clients challenge the limiting belief that focuses on "never having enough" or "never being enough," whether it is related to the concepts of love, accomplishments, acceptance or energy. This negative mindset keeps clients stuck in a helpless state, and prevents them from recognizing their personal qualities, setting appropriate priorities or framing the possibilities for the future in positive terms.

The first is a technique called "The Cloak of Many Colors" which focuses awareness on positive qualities, energies and assets. It is a metaphorical derivation and expansion of the old biblical story of Joseph and his cloak of many colors. In this version, we present the exercise to the client with the following introduction: Joseph's father, Jacob had a unique cloak woven of many fabrics and colors of the time, and gave this to Joseph to show him how special he was, and as an acknowledgment of his many qualities. Each color and fabric represented a different quality. (For the purposes of this exercise, we gloss over the problems that it caused Joseph with his brothers. If clients bring up this idea, they are assured that in this case, no one but them will be able to see or feel this wonderful cloak.)

The first step is to ask the survivor to write a list of all the *things* they really like in their life: memorabilia such as kind notes, cards, presents received, souvenirs or special collections, positive comments that others have made, the "treasures" that nurture them. Then they list the *activities* that are the highlights of their life that gives life meaning: such as sports or recreation, vocational accomplishments or sensual experiences, times when they overcame adversity or disappointment to achieve positive results as well as specific evidence that demonstrate competence and value. Next, they make an extensive, if not exhaustive, list of all the *qualities* they like about themselves. (They may need to ask significant others to share their perceptions of those special qualities.) Clients are then encouraged to list all the *people* in their life who give love, caring, and energy to enhance the quality of life. For those who are literalists, they can keep a copy of these lists with them, taking it out to read whenever they need a 'psychological lift.' For those who are willing or able to engage in a more profound metaphorical experience, we invite them to construct a "Cloak of Many Colors" in their imaginations, using different colors, threads, strands of cloth or fabric to represent *each* of these positive elements in life. They can then imagine that they can *weave* each of these into a large multi-colored cloak which can surround and protect them from perceived emotional hurts or verbal insults. It goes without saying that each person would have a completely different, uniquely constructed and colored protective "cloak." Your client can celebrate her personal uniqueness and practice surrounding herself in that cloak. It is part of what makes her special and human. No one else need know where or when she uses this internal protection and security. It is their personal, internal "security blanket" which allows them to focus on their strengths rather than staying stuck in their perceived limitations.

Following is another metaphor that we use to project the idea that the world is never as limited as we tend to believe it is. We want to shift our client's perceptions about setting relevant priorities which are of great value to her—and to disturb the mortar which cements negative cognitions into place. Like all good metaphors, this one is nested inside of other communications, and after the story is told, no explanation of it is warranted or necessary.

A philosophy professor stood before his class and had some items in front of him. When class began, wordlessly he picked up a large empty mayonnaise jar and proceeded to fill it with rocks about 2" in diameter right to the top. He then asked the students if the jar was full. They agreed that it was. The professor then picked up a box of pebbles and poured them into the jar. He shook the jar lightly. The pebbles of course, rolled into the open areas between the rocks. The students laughed. He asked his students again if the jar was full. Again, they agreed that indeed it was. The professor then picked up a box of sand and poured it into the jar. Of course, the sand filled up everything else.

"Now," said the professor, "I want you to recognize that this is your life. The rocks are the important things—your family, your partner, your health, and your children—anything that is so important to you that if it were lost, you would be nearly destroyed. The pebbles are the other things in life that matter, but on a smaller scale. The pebbles represent things like your job, house, or car. The sand is everything else, the small stuff."

"If you put the sand or the pebbles into the jar first, there is no room for the rocks. The same goes for your life. If you spend all your energy and time on the small stuff, the material things, you will never have room for the things that are truly most important."

"Pay attention to the things that are critical in your life. Play with your children. Take time to get medical checkups. Take your partner out dancing. There will always be time to go to work, clean the house, give a dinner party and fix the disposal. Take care of the rocks first—the things that really matter. Set your priorities, the rest is just pebbles and sand."

The concepts explored in the next chapter relate to integrating that healed inner child with a competent, well-functioning adult ego state who can function effectively in the world of work, responsibility and achievement. Establishing competent interpersonal relationships is the next great challenge for these clients.

[7]

Integrating the Functional Adult with the Healed Inner Child

Healing from sexual abuse involves reclaiming those lost aspects of the self, picking up the pieces that are left behind. It is often the "inner child" who stores those lost memories and feelings on behalf of the adult. Trauma, pain and rigid conditioning forced the natural, innocent, carefree part of the developing child underground. This inner child is repressed and hard to reach. On a conscious level, the client has survived, adapted to successive events and experiences and matured with adult understanding and logic, while in great measure, the "inner child" has been neither validated nor healed. It is as if this inner child has carried the burden of secrecy, guilt, insecurity, and self-reproach. Listening with an intuitive ear to the concerns of the client, we can allow them the covert permission to retrieve and release the memories which have been protectively pent up. When this pain has been honored and validated, the adult survivor is freed from using limiting and obsolete survival strategies. The metaphor of the "Inner Child" is useful in exploring and helping to heal the hurt inside that at times is incomprehensible. It also can help in reclaiming their sense of innocence and playfulness that is typically experienced in a normative childhood.

Penelope, at age 35, had been married for ten years with two children. She came in for counseling complaining about relationship problems created by her intense crying spells and outbursts of anger which she could not control or explain, but which she describes as similar to the temper tantrums her children display.

99

These intense emotions were having an adverse impact both on her marriage which she wanted to save, and on the well being of her two small children. She had physically matured by age nine. She had been very close to her father, and was considered "his favorite." There was a great deal of tension and marital conflict in the home while Penelope was growing up. When the father, Leon, complained that Penelope's mother was "making his life miserable," Penelope was sympathetic. Leon took advantage of her compassion and continued to "break down in tears" in his daughters presence. Leon became more expressive on how appreciative he was for the attention Penelope paid to his concerns. He spoke about how he felt unloved and lonely in his marriage, and how different it was when Penelope responded with caring and support for his concerns. Leon's apparent need for reassurance eventually turned to physical affection, as he told his daughter that she was the only reason he was staying in the marriage. Penelope made a decision that she was now responsible for salvaging what she perceived as the stability and well-being of her family. As she reached her mid-teens, she became aware that the intimate relationship with her father was inappropriate. Her mother ignored her allegations, shrugged her shoulders and made comments about her imagination "running away with her." Her father vehemently denied that he ever did anything wrong, causing Penelope to question her own reality about her family dynamics. Leon concocted rationales to punish her or deny her privileges to go out with friends or to attend parties.

She became increasingly uncomfortable around her father and angry at her mother, who attributed Penelope's change in mood and behavior as just "being a difficult teenager." Penelope worked hard in high school so that she could qualify for a scholarship to college far from home. Leon insisted he could not afford to send her away to school. She realized it for the ruse it was to keep her close to home and tied to him. She succeeded in obtaining a full scholarship at the college of her choice and enjoyed the freedom of being away from home. She described her dating life as filled with "one-night stands" and unsatisfying relationships. After many failed attempts, Penelope finally met a man who treated her with patience, honesty, and respect and was someone whom she thought she could love. They dated for over a year before they married.

How we worked together to help her to acknowledge and value the reality of her perceptions that had been distorted is the part of the healing process that will be discussed throughout this chapter. We focused on identifying the traumatic triggers which initiated her crying spells and angry outbursts. She recognized that when she feels dismissed or manipulated by others in her life, she becomes negatively reactive in childish ways. The relationship between traumatic childhood experiences and her presenting complaints became clear when she recognized how closely analogous situations in the present where she felt that manipulated or dismissed by others, were to the emotions she experienced in her childhood when her father used pretense and rationalization to exploit her, and her mother minimized her allegations. Penelope needed guidance to replay her childhood with a positive outcome that was facilitated by developing an older wiser self (inner advisor) who helped her reclaim her real perceptions of the intrusiveness of her father's behavior on her life. The necessity to grow up quickly to stabilize the dysfunction of her family took from Penelope the experiences, reactions and behaviors appropriate to a developing, nurtured child.

Over the course of the years, many abuse survivors have developed strengths, skills and resources which have allowed them to function appropriately in many areas of their life. We want them to recognize what they have accomplished that can be viewed as good, or healthy, or competent. This assists our clients to get past the perception that their very identities are defined by victimhood. We help them "turn the lemons into lemonade," by transforming their ill-conceived liabilities into valuable assets. When we introduce even small changes into their identified habitual behavior patterns, that now are focused on a positive outcome instead of operating inside the paradigm of the problem, they can see that they are moving towards future progress, resolution and healing.

When we introduce the concept of incorporating a positive frame of reference to our clients, some have expressed a sense of relief that there is now a plausible explanation that they can easily accept of how they can be doing so well on the surface, yet are so tormented inside with conflicting intense emotions and inappropriate behaviors. In cases of extreme or continual abuse, the child part sometimes splits off entirely. While an appropriate survival mechanism, this dissociation can become so well organized, it sometimes results in dissociative identity disorder.

As we create the concept of an inner child, we allow the survivor to metaphorically step into a position of an older, mature, and wise mentor to an impotent, naïve younger self. It is in this role that the healing of the scars of the abuse can take place. The abused "inner child" is experientially brought into the treatment in the context of our supportive therapeutic environment. The adult can accept, validate and encourage this inner child who has been so badly damaged. She then discovers the self-validation for her experiences in her new adult context and grieves for what was lost.

The client, herself, learns how to validate the experiences that others whom she trusted forced her to have. One of the strongest psychological messages perpetrators impose on many youngsters is that:

> To survive, you must deny this experience; in other words, deny everything about yourself. Therefore you can't trust what your experience and senses tell you are true. You have to adapt to this new reality which may mean lying or dissembling to survive. No one will believe you if you tell anyway.

This is one way these limiting ego beliefs were created. Young people do not have the logic, wisdom or experience to effectively combat the formation of these beliefs.

They also did not have an advocate either to intercede on their behalf or to make their reality understandable. These survivors may need a "coach" or "mentor" to encourage them to be strong, validated and independent. As clinicians, we can invite them to create an internal support system or "mentor." This internal "mentor" invents perhaps the only persona who can truly understands exactly what that younger inner child victim had experienced; the *only* one who can validate and nurture that inner child. This allows the client to take control of the healing process, saying what that inner child needs to hear, in the tone of voice that will ensure that the words will be heard. "Mentors" can be fanciful or practical, limited only by imagination. One client generated an image of a large English-speaking dog, who could hear all her pain, reassure her and love her unconditionally. He would always protect her from anyone who would ever hurt her again. Not only did she imagine that she was safe, but she could think of her special "mentor," giggle, and have a lighthearted moment. Another client created her own very wise, nurturing "fairy god-mother." This gives the client all the time necessary to heal at an individual rate and pace. Basically we are allying with the inner child who now can feel cared for, protected and thoroughly understood. Consequently, the inner child participates in an implicit agreement to accept the positive changes that healing offers.

There are many ways to encourage the client to reconnect positively with the child within. By no means are we suggesting that using any of the following is a necessity for effective therapy. These are methods that we have found helpful particularly when the therapy process seems to get bogged down in minutiae, or when the client is stymied on what to do to connect with and reassure the wounded inner child. Usually this evolves later in the therapeutic process. The exercises stimulate the creative energies in clients and they often report that these tasks are "more fun" than they thought therapy would be. You might want to create an appropriate adaptation of any of the suggestions offered. Each has its own energy, timing and unique appeal to individual clients. They are presented below as you might present them to your client along with the rationale for using them.

1. **Bring in photo albums, pictures or videotapes if appropriate or available. Compare a picture of you as a younger child before the abuse occurred to one which was taken afterwards.** Collaborate with the client to take notice of any objective differences in the pictures such as posture, expressions, activities portrayed or environment. The therapeutic value lies in the connotations or implications of these differences, and what they mean to the client. It is an opportunity to point out the innocence and positive energy of that younger child before she was subjected to that abusive behavior. It is the positive energy to which the client is entitled, and which must be reclaimed.

2. **Write a letter to yourself as a child—tell her how wonderful she is and that she never deserved to be hurt. Validate the reality of the hurt. Give permission to grieve and mourn the loss of her innocence.** It was neither her fault nor her responsibility that it happened regardless of what she was told. Reassure her that she *has* survived—and did the best she could with the resources she had under the circumstances. The reality is that she will continue to survive that abuse. Remind her that indeed it *did* come to an end. Never again will she be subjected to that abuse. This intervention

externalizes the pain, and accesses the clients own capacity to provide nurturing and self-care.

3. **Create an imaginary scene of your life as a child the way it always should have been. Imagine a safe childhood peopled with kind, loving, protective adults.** Think about what would be different, and what appropriate beliefs you would be building about yourself and your place in the world. Step into that scene and feel the feelings associated with it. A variation on this is to imagine you as your child's parent, knowing exactly what to say or to do that would have made a difference in your life. Creating and imagining these scenes is an implicit permission for the client to feel differently about herself, and adopt a positive frame of reference as well as an appropriate forward-looking orientation to accomplishing goals in her future.

4. **With the help of friends, or in a group, create a drama or fantasy about your childhood. You can have someone else role-play you as a child, while as a "visitor from her future," you can reassure her that she is competent, beautiful, lovable, cared about and that everything is going to turn out just fine. Reverse roles and feel the comfort presented to you in your own words.** This takes a page from the "Psychodrama" theory of healing which pulls on the energy and comfort of a group, and allows the wounded child within to hear the words of comfort from her "protective adult ego" in another person's voice. This gives it some objectivity, validity and legitimacy which sometimes make it easier for the client to take in.

5. **Create a scene where you return to the scene of the abuse as your adult self, protecting the child by standing up to the perpetrator.** You can take along all the allies or reinforcements you like, but you need to be your own hero. Many survivors have said that they wished they could have had the courage to have faced down the abuser, even though rationally, they realized they could not have succeeded. Being assertive may have even generated grave danger from the perpetrator. They will now have permission to verbalize the frustration, anger, outrage, grief, or disgust which has been building up inside them for those many years.

6. **Learn new ways to play. Experiment with different positive recreational activities. Dare to be silly and sponta-**

neous. Many survivors have been saddled with expectations from others of being responsible, holding things together, and taking a serious outlook on life. They simply do not have permission to relax, express humor or have fun. As a homework assignment, which of course, they *will* take seriously, ask them to create five to ten ways of having fun or being silly, and report what these are at the next appointment. Now you can invite them to experiment engaging in at least four of them and discover which of them is the most enjoyable. (This implies that at least one of them will be.) You can predict that they will find this task difficult to do. This very difficulty is an indication of how much it is needed. Increase their motivation for accomplishing the task. There is nothing like playfulness to bring out the positive resources of the child within.

7. **Use affirmations to heal the inner child. In a safe, quiet, relaxed setting, imagine that you are sitting and talking to the child/person you were at the time of the abuse.** These are positive, self statements that affirm the value and worth of the client at the core of her being in spite of having been abused. Invite the client to create others which are personal and appropriate. Repeat each statement of affirmation both aloud and silently until the "inner child' accepts each as her own:

    - The sexual abuse was not my fault.
    - I am a valuable and good person.
    - I am not bad because of what happened.
    - My feelings and responses during the abuse were normal, understandable and protective.
    - My sexual energy is good and separate from the abuse.
    - I am a strong, competent person.
    - I can share my pain and hurt with others, and it can become less.

"Shawn" was a 45-year-old divorcee who came to counseling after her third marriage ended with much recrimination after five rocky years. Devastated, she believed she must be an evil or disturbed person to have attracted and fallen for so many abusive men who took advantage of her vulnerabilities, and left her alone and financially strapped. Shawn is a unique, creative individual who loves crafts such as cross stitch, weaving, macramé, designing and sewing her own clothes, but does not respond well to working at a salaried job, which feeds into her vulnerability to criticism. Consequently, she has leaned on men as a means of financial support.

Growing up, Shawn and her two older sisters were neglected emotionally, and upon further inquiry, she reported that her father had molested her over a period of four years, in addition to continually disparaging and criticizing her for any perceived misconduct or performance over the course of her childhood. She was called, "the crazy daughter of the family" and ignored or dismissed. Shawn remembered her mother as being weak and submissive to the father, and had refused to confront him, even though all the girls complained about his mistreatment. As far as Shawn knew, she had been the only one in the family who had been molested.

Filled with self-doubt and personal recrimination, she had bought into her father's disdain and ridicule. He screamed at her about grades, so she did not do well in high school, and never even attempted college.

During our therapy together, using several Solution-Focused and Ericksonian approaches, Shawn was able to recognize that she was a victim with no responsibility in the molestation, regardless of the ridicule that the perpetrator heaped on her. She was then able to release some of the anger, sadness and fear about asserting herself. Shawn replayed her childhood in her imagination from the time she was born and held in her "ideal" mother's arms, who assured her that she was loved, special and now celebrated her uniqueness. She replayed her "ideal" father as someone who would only protect and respect her as well as encourage her energy and creativity. She integrated these positive evaluations inside and enjoyed the energy and thoughts that evolved from them. She was excited about the realizations and insights about her childhood that developed as a result of her therapeutic work. One of her insights was that the father had been severely beaten and punished as a child, and understood few other ways of relating to anybody else, particularly children. Towards the end of his life, although he never apologized for the sexual abuse, he mellowed as a critic. He told her he loved her and was glad she was his daughter. As if out of a page in Shakespeare's *King Lear*, Shawn was at his bedside to take care of him when her mother became incapacitated, and her two sisters refused to have much to do with him. She felt very good about herself and her capacity to take care of her father. Shawn integrated a sense of her personal qualities and values in which she could take great pride, and began to formulate her own set of goals. While they still did not involve working for an employer, she started a craft consulting business to help others learn to discover their own creative skills.

Once positive healing of the wounds of the sexual abuse has been integrated, the survivor can focus on behavioral adaptations to life independent of the therapeutic relationship. The preparation for the eventual and inevitable termination of therapy is designed to increase the client's recognition of competence and self esteem. The suggestions included in the following chapter will help in easing the transition.

[8]

Termination of Therapy

Giving the Process Meaning

Into every successful (or even unsuccessful) therapeutic relationship comes the inevitability of the termination of the sessions. We face a challenge of how to accomplish this predictable and necessary step in the recovery process of the client. In the best of therapy situations, it is difficult to plan the ending of treatment. It is particularly challenging when working with abuse or incest survivors. There is a tendency for this particular class of clients, who may have been denied validation and nurturing throughout their traumatic experiences and its aftermath, to cling to caregivers who listen to them intently and have offered the much needed validation and support. Care must be taken to insure these very vulnerable clients do not feel abandoned as the final sessions near. Awareness of the inevitability of the eventual ending of this therapeutic connection is necessary regardless of how long therapy has been going on.

CONFRONTATION AND DISCLOSURE

The idea of closure of treatment for many of our clients often initiates a dilemma about whether of not appropriate healing is possible without confronting the perpetrator or disclosing the reality of the abuse to other family members. Is it possible to move on without "forgiveness" of the perpetrator or "acknowledgment" of the immense harm caused to the survivor by the abuser? Even if these ideas were raised during the course of therapy, as treatment winds down, there is renewed anxiety about these issues. We like to believe that every survivor, if given the chance, knows what is inherently best for her. These choices are filtered through each client's unique experiences, her current life circumstances, value system, spirituality, or particularly any personal intuition regarding the potential outcomes. The appropriate therapeutic response to these questions is perceived neutrality, and non-judgment.

It is important to recognize that confrontation does not start the process of recovery. It is the result and culmination of much consideration and preparation. Just as a builder would never enter into a project without first obtaining the proper tools and having the skills to use them, patients should not be encouraged to proceed with a confrontation until they have thoroughly explored their own motives and goals, and until they have prepared themselves emotionally for the reactions they may provoke.

Confrontations with the perpetrator or family member should never be considered the final outcome of treatment. There are many circumstances where confrontation is contra-indicated because of the potential for physical harm. We must never underestimate this potential when helping our clients to consider disclosure or confrontation.

The following concepts should be considered thoroughly before clients attempt to engage in any confrontation with abusers:

1. Do it to honor your feelings.
2. Do it only *because you* want to, *when you* want to. Only you can decide if and when.
3. Do it from a position of strength. Don't go into the experience expecting an acknowledgment and/or apology from the perpetrator. Don't expect the family to absolve any guilt you might feel.
4. Thoroughly examine your expectations and all possible outcomes. The more prepared you are, the stronger you will be before, during and after the confrontation experience.
5. If possible, use factual details in your discussion. Although it is not necessary for healing to occur, it assists in validating your belief of yourself.
6. Do not let the abuser apologize too quickly or too easily. "No pain—no gain" for him.
7. If other abuse survivors are in the family, mutual or group confrontation may strengthen you resolve or position. On the other hand, no one should be pressured into participation.

8. Get the necessary emotional support you need, both for the preparation as well as the aftermath of the confrontation.

Herman (1981) describes the role of preparation and the possible benefits of confrontation: Once adequate preparation has been done, the confrontation can be an important milestone in the patient's mastery of the incest trauma. It can be a kind of rite in which the patients sheds her identity as a "witch," "bitch," or "whore" and casts off her role as the guardian of the family secret. She does not expect her family to absolve her of her guilt; rather, she *absolves herself in their presence*. If family members respond with denial, panic, hostility, or threats, the survivor is encouraged to observe these reactions and to judge from them how powerful those same family pressures must have been on her when she was a child. (Herman, 1981, 193–194)

The decision to confront should *never* be imposed on a survivor, particularly to meet the agenda or needs of the therapist. We should support and offer reassurance to our client regardless of her decision about confrontation and disclosure. We must be clear in our discussion of this issue that the client's resistance or decision not to confront and disclose should in no way affect on the client's or therapist's perception of the overall successfulness of the therapy. It should be pointed out to the client that many positive therapeutic outcomes have been accomplished without a confrontation.

The need to be seen as "right," often by the very people who instigated or tolerated the abuse, is so important to some survivors that they will compromise their own realities.

There are those who still wait for someone else to tell them that they are right before they can feel whole again. Those who wait for validation from their abusers are waiting for the impossible. A simple apology doesn't make them feel all right. Someone telling you that they understand how you feel seems shallow and insincere, and doesn't make it right.

Confronting the offender along with any others the survivor holds responsible for sexual abuse does not mean that they have to admit that she's right, or even "OK" for healing to take place.

Maggie was a 17-year-old adolescent, who was court ordered to attend counseling after she disclosed a history of sexual abuse by her father consisting of sexual intercourse three or four times a week. As Maggie's therapy continued, she developed a greater understanding of how her mother had unconsciously known that her father had been abusing her for many years. During a session of dyad treatment with her mother, Maggie confronted her mother, "Joan," with the fact that Joan knew what happened. Joan became outraged and left the room. Mainly because our (Mark) work together taught her to validate her own reality, Maggie was not offended by her mother's ignorance and defensiveness.

As the therapy progressed, she was able to get her validation from an unlikely resource. There was an opportunity for Maggie, her mother, and her father to be in the same therapy room. Maggie took this opportunity to once again confront her mother with the fact that Joan knew that her father was molesting her. As expected, her mother once again denied this reality and Maggie went on to remind her of a specific example.

"Mom, remember the time that we were driving on the turnpike, and you were driving in the front with my two sisters; and Dad and I were sitting in the back. Remember how you looked in the rear view mirror, and saw Dad and I having sex in the back seat. You just simply shook your head and continue to drive."

Predictably Maggie's mother denied this truth as well. This time, however, her father stated, *"She's absolutely right. You looked, you shook your head—and you kept on driving."* Maggie's abuser now became her ally and her "voice of truth." Even with this information, Maggie's mother would not or could not accept any role in her daughter's abuse. Maggie knew that she had spoken the truth, had dealt with it effectively, and was ready to move on *even without her mother's permission.*

Although Maggie's story is an example of success, most confrontations are in fact unsatisfying as they are often met by denial or negative outcomes.

We must be mindful not to superimpose our belief system onto the client. One of our most important values that could be the most helpful to clients is that during the course of therapy, they have learned that not only are they capable of making the "correct" decisions, but we believe in them.

THE PROCESS OF TERMINATION

Inevitably, therapy must come to a close. There is a mixture of emotions for client and therapist alike. Many survivors may know when it is time to leave treatment and will initiate termination conversations. As in any therapeutic process, this should be a gradual, weaning process. It is important to allow survivors a good deal of control over the ending process: when to end, how to end, and some sense of what will happen when it's over. This process allows the client to anticipate and understand how they have come full circle from a position of dependency and victimization to one of empowerment and control.

Specifically, one way we can accomplish this is by encouraging and verifying their accomplishments in the therapy process. We can offer reassurance to our clients that the opportunity and ability to return to therapy is always available. It is certainly reasonable to predict there will be times in the future when she may need to talk as new issues develop or perhaps she may recognize the need to do further work regarding her abuse. This statement of options and availability allows even the most complicated and difficult terminations of therapy to proceed relatively smoothly.

> I work with clients as long as it takes for them to experience relief from symptoms, resolution of the intrusive traumatic memories, and acquisition of a hopeful and non-symptomatic orientation towards the future. (Dolan, p. 203)

In many situations, I (Jill) begin this termination process in the first session by acknowledging that our time together is precious, whether or not the number of sessions is limited by insurance companies. In setting therapeutic goals and by specifying the criteria for achieving those goals early in the process, we are already setting up the parameters for terminating our work together. There are several important questions we can ask that are potential predictors to the success of treatment. They provide the best criteria and evidence of specifically knowing what will be happening when the goals are nearing accomplishment and that we are reaching an end to our sessions. In other words, at the beginning of treatment, the client is framing the work into the future by focusing on what they want to do or will do in treatment. By posing the question *"How will you know when our work together will be completed?"* or *"What will you be doing, saying or feeling when your goals are met?"* We are thus implicitly setting the stage for getting and recognizing achievement of a successful outcome. The issues and/or difficulties that brought our clients into therapy are now redefined as remediable. This approach also gives the client the expectation that there are important and necessary steps in the process of accomplishing their goals, as well as the implicit permission to make the necessary changes to accomplish them. We empower our clients to cherish their independence and their strengths.

Toward the end of each intervention, we invite the client to check inside their conscious awareness for any concerns, considerations, or objections to incorporating the new behaviors or changes they have made. This helps them take ownership of those skills. If necessary, they are encouraged to make any adjustments required, taking into account their unique circumstances from an emotional and/or the physical environments in which they live. This ensures that the new behaviors they are trying out are appropriate to the complexities of their lives. They can rehearse how they will be using the skills and new responses into their imagined future. This makes their new behaviors relevant and practical outside the perceived protection of our office or our nurturing presence.

The process of ending therapy should include a review of all the good work accomplished. The client and therapist have an opportunity, and perhaps the responsibility, to do a reality check and express their own points of view about the nature of the progress that has been made. We can draw the analogy and summon up the memories of our client when she first entered treatment, and her personal impressions of how she is feeling and responding differently now.

These contrasts serve to bolster the client's self-perceptions of her sense of growth. While it is important to look at accomplishments, we can also point out the potential "hot spots" and triggers that can still exist for our client. The objective is to let the client know she is "new and improved" but not necessarily perfect. If the client is given the message that she is "fixed" and no longer vulnerable to return to her old ways, she may be set up for disappointment at the least and disillusionment and feelings of betrayal at the worst. We need to encourage a discussion of potential pitfalls or imagined barriers or sabotages which may occur, and the "plan B" strategies to cope with these eventualities. We can therefore acknowledge and validate that while certain issues are volatile, she has all the resources available to manage them as they arise.

As soon as the necessary work has been accomplished, we can reassure our client that her needs will be respected if she desires or requires further sessions. Termination, in and of itself, does not need to be a problem. If there is some concern or hesitation from the client, this may give us an objective description of what the next step in the counseling could be. Since our intention is always to make our clients independent of our services, it is a cooperative decision on how and when this takes place, as well as what is needed to make that possible.

If a client is in group treatment with other survivors, and decides to terminate, she is asked to tell the group of her decision during one session and is expected to return for an additional session. This request allows time to:

1. Discuss the reasons for leaving,
2. Explore any misperceptions or break downs in communication,
3. Give each member opportunities to share reactions,
4. Give and receive feedback,
5. Gain some degree of closure, and to say goodbye.

I (Mark) have observed that, frequently, after the process unfolds during this "last session" the client chooses to remain in the group, especially if her reason for leaving was based on her own sensitivity, hyper-vigilance, or any type of distorted belief systems regarding her "value" to the group, such as *"I don't make a difference to the group." "This work is too painful, and it doesn't matter anyway because I am who I am, and nothing will change."* My observations lec me to proceed with this "one last session rule" where any distorted beliefs could be addressed, understood and remedied.

It is clear that most of you reading this would stand firm in the belief that social relationships with our clients after treatment has concluded is not a good idea, either for therapist or client. I (Mark) have heard countless stories that there still remain clinicians who initiate and maintain non-therapeutic associations, many times including sexual relations. This "switch" in alliances from therapist to friend (or worse) can be particularly damaging for survivors, because of the potential for replicating the lack of boundaries and betrayal of trust which were found in their families of origin. A more appropriate, professional, post-treatment kind of relationship with a client that may offer some positive outcomes is one where the client continues to keep the therapist informed about her progress perhaps through holiday cards or little notes, as time goes by. In this way, the client can perceive being in control of reducing some of the abandonment issues relevant to ending therapy or left over from experiences with other significant people in her life. This is particularly true for those survivors who have confronted their perpetrators and/or family of origin and been ostracized by them, thus cutting off communication or contact. A supportive, *brief* response from a therapist after receiving a note or card can be meaningful. It is a positive reinforcement of all the good work the client has been doing. In no manner am I advocating continuing therapy by mail, (or e-mail or instant messaging). However, I think it can be very helpful and supportive for the client to include an occasional contact with the therapist inside the boundaries of what is acceptable and appropriate.

> I have often wondered why these patients keep seeking help despite repeated failures and disappointments. One might view this behavior as simply another repetition compulsion. Or, taking a more affirmative view, one might consider their persistence as a testimony to their virtues of determination and hope. Many of us who work with these patients have been inspired by their courage. Their endurance in the pursuit of treatment reflects a conviction, often unarticulated but nonetheless very powerful, that recovery can begin if only the right connection—between patient and caregiver, and between symptoms and trauma-can be found. Our role in the healing process is to bear witness and thus to make it possible for the patient to bear a reality that cannot be borne in isolation. By our presence, we enable our patients to tell what has happened to them and to make sense of the unspeakable events of the past. (Herman, 1990, page 291)

In summary, we can help our clients prepare for ending our therapeutic relationship in healthy and productive ways to allow continued growth, healing and further development. The mutual sharing of the good work done by both therapist and client allows both to feel proud of their perseverance, and to appreciate their individual resiliency. The next case study presents an illustration that some of the best healing work is accomplished by the client outside of the therapy room, after the major interpersonal counseling work was complete.

Teresa came to treatment shortly after she had confronted her memories of being sexually abused by her father over a three year period. Before her memories had surfaced, Teresa had been extremely involved with her family. She lived in the same town as her parents, and her children were in regular contact with their grandparents. As treatment progressed, Teresa was becoming more empowered to confront her family and identify how she felt about what had happened.

The following is a letter she wrote to her parents, expressing her feelings and contemplations while incorporating the many ideas that had surfaced for her in treatment including the potency of secrets, and illusions. Her writings are an indication of the powerful energy, persistence and strength that survivors are capable of achieving, working within a collaborative, solution-focused treatment model that respects, validates, and acknowledges the client's memories and experiences.

> "I'm standing in the middle of two generations.
> I can't face my parents and heal it that way.
> Maybe I can turn to my children and heal it in
> the other direction.
> That would be making an end to it"

Mom and Dad,

Steve has asked me more than once what he can give me for my birthday. This year, it's time for me to give myself a birthday present, one more valuable, more painful, than anything I could imagine.

This year I give myself life; a new beginning, a chance to find out, for the first time, exactly who I am. Not who I should be, not who someone else thinks I am, but the real me. I don't know the real me. My feelings, my true self, have been buried deep inside for years—for as long as I can remember. All I know is I'm filled with anger, shame, pain and a whole mixed up bunch of emotions that have just settled on the inside because of a secret. Because of something that never should have happened because of sexual abuse.

To you Dad, I give you back the pain. I've carried it with me an entire lifetime, and now it's yours. I don't want i. You abused me; you caused me harm. My own father, who was supposed to keep me from harm, was the harm. You say you love me, you care about me. You are the source of the problem. You want to help. You can't; it's not good enough. The harm is already done, the pain already real. You take it, you take it all. I don't want it anymore ever. I forgive myself now for keeping the secret, for feeling it was my responsibility to keep it, to protect you, to protect everyone. It wasn't my responsibility, it was yours. I was a child. I was not the cause of the pain, you were. It is rightfully yours.

Mom, you are my mother, you were supposed to take care of me, protect me and you didn't. I believe you knew what was going on and chose not to help me, but chose dad instead. And still do. You live there with him, waiting for me to tell you what to do. Get your own help to deal with your own struggles. I am not your support. I am not your answer. I am not your forgiveness. None of this is for me to give, for I am not the problem. I was the victim, and now the survivor. Every action has its consequences.

For my 34th birthday, I give myself the gift of healing, the gift of going on to a healthy, happy life. I give myself dreams, feelings truth. I give my husband, my children, those same dreams, feelings, and truth. The secret I have kept with me has had devastating and lasting effects. Now it's over.

No more secrets. No more lies—just the truth. I'm giving up a wish for security and protection, for everything to be safe. I'm giving up the hope that some how, some day, a miracle will come true and my family will come through for me. It's too late for that. It's too late for many things. I'm scared. Scared of being out there without my parents, scared of being alone, relying on myself to take care of me. Scared of giving up the family I've come to know. Although it's not what it appears to be. The pictures in my mind, the yearning in my heart of what my family could be is not the one I have. It never has been. How could anyone let that happen? I just don't understand.

Now I have my own family, a husband and two children who mean the world to me. I will not continue to live a lie with my family. My life is going to be true for me, not for anyone else. I will not let my children's lives be a lie. I will not let things continue as they are, pretending that things are the way they aren't. My children are too precious to me to include them in the continuation of a secret. They will not be part of a secret. Secrets destroy. Silence destroys. I should know.

I do not want any contact with you. I am putting up some walls around me, to protect me, to allow me to heal myself and to find myself without outside interference. I can't afford to allow myself to be affected by pretense, by tradition, by false beliefs, by the origin of the pain. It's not right. It doesn't feel right. I have to feel right.

I'm setting myself free—Freedom! What a wonderful thing. I'll soar. I know I will. You've raised a strong daughter.

Teresa

[9]

Shifting Our Perspective

Issues of Covert Sexual Abuse and Sibling Incest

In the treatment of survivors of incest, there are two specific groups of survivors, that are frequently overlooked or dismissed as being "less affected" than other survivors. These are the people who have been exposed to *covert sexual abuse,* and those who were involved in *sibling abuse.* Below is a discussion of these client populations that deserve consideration when conducting assessment and treatment with clients.

COVERT SEXUAL ABUSE

Many clinicians working with survivors of sexual abuse are comfortable recognizing the aftereffects of such abuse on clients who can describe a childhood "memory" or understanding of *specific and direct* sexual contact within the dynamics of a familial relationship. We understand the potential longer term effects of *Overt Sexual Abuse.* However, there are fewer clinicians who are familiar with the impact of *Covert Sexual Abuse.*

Covert abuse is more specific to the relationship between a child and a parent. It occurs when a child becomes identified or represents an object of the parent's affection, passion or preoccupation. The parent, often driven by their lack of age-appropriate relationships and needs, elevates their child to a new relationship status, where the child is frequently viewed as an equal, in a collaborative relationship or partnership, resembling a more age-defined relationship. The child's reality is blurred regarding the appropriate

119

parental boundaries that should be seen as nurturing and care-taking versus those exhibited where the sense of seduction and enmeshment is present and pervasive. A role reversal occurs in which the needs of the child to differentiate, and eventually separate to an independent individual, are subjugated to the parent's need to have a "partner." Feeling the lack of alternatives, the child feels continually "caught in a web" of entangled emotions and needs of their demanding/seductive parent. This distortion of appropriate boundaries and expectations dramatically alters the normative developmental stages including sexual identity and development.

While survivors of overt sexual abuse usually carry memory of the physical sexual activity, covert abuse survivors have no conscious memory of the physical sexual contact, thus they rarely identify themselves as sexual abuse survivors.

"Roger," a 28 year old single man, presented for treatment with relationship issues, particularly with women who are interested in pursuing a "physical" relationship. He stated that he had been unable to proceed with a sexual relationship, as he had an overwhelming feeling of dread and being out of control. He also disclosed recurring complaints of being afraid to enter his townhouse in the evenings, experiencing a pervasive sense of being unsafe. He told of several occasions where he would sit outside his townhouse, for prolonged periods of time, waiting for a roommate to return home. He also stated that if the wait became too long, he would retrieve a hunting knife from his car. This afforded him some security to enter the house.

As the initial interview progressed, he also described a history of overwhelming nightmares and insomnia. He related that he had feeling of "someone" entering his room at night, and reaching under the covers. He could not recall what happened next, but he insinuated that he felt that someone may have touched him inappropriately. His image of the "someone" consisted solely of an arm and hand, no other body parts, particularly no face to offer an identity to the individual. As he recounted his history, he reported that for several years, his mother had a relationship with him that Roger defined as "unusual." He described his mother as particularly solicitous of his presence for visits, for help and advice. He noticed that this seemed to occur when his father was away from the family home on business. Roger's mother would invite him to her home for dinner and present in what Roger saw as flirtatious and inappropriate. "She would get dressed up in clothes that would seem out of place for a casual dinner at home." Further exploration indicated numerous occasions when the family would go out for dinner, and his mother would sit next to him. At least once during each dinner, Roger would find his mother placing her hand on his leg, under the table, out of sight of his father and other family members. He felt uncomfortable, but did not ask her to stop, for fear of causing embarrassment to his mother or himself.

As treatment progressed, Roger was still experiencing the same intrusive nightmares and sleep disruption. Through the use of a mild trance state, Roger was able to visualize sleeping in his own bed, when someone enters the room. With increasing support, and utilization of a "safety anchor," he was able to eventually see a clearer image of the situation. What he saw was his mother entering the room, and coming to his bed. She would straighten his sheets, tucking him in. Roger recalls waking one time and seeing his mother in the room by his bed, as she was mumbling, "It's just me, checking to make sure you're OK. Dad's away and I'm lonely."

She proceeded to get into his bed, and "snuggled" with him until morning. He remembered feeling that this was "not natural,—my mother shouldn't be in my bed." He did not recall any specific sexual contact.

Treatment continued with Roger feeling increasingly confident that the relationship with his mother was contributory to fears of entering his townhouse and his relationship difficulties. He identified a fear of entering his house, precipitated by an eerie sense that someone was waiting for him. He was able to articulate an impression that the women he was dating, and with whom he wanted to get physical, were triggering a sense of defectiveness in him, because of his "unusual" relationship he had with his mother. With continued support, Roger was able to confront his mother's current interactions with him and the perception that she was seductive and intrusive. On one occasion, while his father was away, his mother invited him to go out for dinner. When he arrived at the family home, his mother came out of the house.

She was dressed in what Roger described as "fancy clothes that were inappropriate for dinner at a local restaurant; and made-up like she was going out on a *date*." She got into the car and slid across the seat and sat right next to Roger. He describes immediately feeling uneasy, and after pulling away from the curb, he just as quickly turned the car around, pulled back to the driveway and told his mother, "The *date* is over. Please leave."

After mild protestation, his mother left the car and went inside the house. Several days later, Roger did confront his mother about his beliefs and feelings. Despite her denials of the reasons behind her behavior, she couldn't deny the intensity of Roger feelings, or how the relationship would have to change.

Roger continued in treatment, and indeed the relationship with his mother did change. There were clearer boundaries set-up and Roger reported a dramatic reduction in the nightmares and intrusive feelings. He resumed dating, but still carried some minor discomfort when things could turn sexual. However, with increasing awareness, he was not scared to try to connect with these women.

Despite the differences in the "memory" of physical contact, many of the symptoms that survivors of covert abuse present are similar to those of survivors of overt sexual abuse. During assessment, they report the following feelings and belief systems:

- Confusion about sexual norms
- Negative feelings associated with sexual activities and arousal sensations
- Lowered self-esteem
- Issues of dependency
- Mistrust of intimates and others
- Anxiety and fear
- Impaired ability to trust one's own judgment.

Behaviorally, they report some of the following:

- Absence of sexual feelings and desire
- Sexual dysfunction
- Difficulty with establishing rewarding partner relationships and commitments
- Fear and rejection of intimacy
- Issues of co-dependency
- Problems with decision making
- Depression
- Suicidal

Regarding treatment, working with survivors of reported covert abuse is challenging. Many come for treatment for a multitude of reporting issues. As the concept of possible covert abuse is explored, they struggle with defining and becoming aware of the incestuous bond between them and the offending parent. For many this is the biggest block to their recovery. Because they frequently lack any conscious knowledge of the physical/sexual boundary intrusion, the survivor is more likely to stay focused on specific symptom relief or resolution rather than allow their belief system or their model of the world to include a more inclusive view of the family situation.

No confirmed negative identity as the guardian of a malignant secret is identified by such survivors as is typically seen with the survivors of overt abuse. They did not think of themselves as irreparably evil or damaged, and do not feel doomed to exclusion from "normal" society because of their secret.

With this reluctance to look at the incestuous bond, treatment needs to begin with an increasing awareness of the incestuous dynamics in their specific parent/child relationships, as well as the boundary intrusions inherent in these relationships. Discussion of healthier child development and the expected emancipation process is often useful. Frequently, the contrast between what is defined as a normative development and their reported experiences is sufficient to demonstrate the presence of abuse for the client, and open up a greater understanding of the possible causes for their presenting symptoms.

Since many covert abuse survivors have never identified the possible source of their present undesired behaviors or feelings, they often revert to the cognitive distortion that the source of their present dissatisfaction with their life circumstances is inherent inside of them rather than imposed on their psyche by others. The need to interpret present behavior within the context of understanding the dynamics of covert sexual abuse helps the survivor to realistically differentiate both the damage incurred, and the opportunities for creating new options for change.

After defining and understanding the boundary intrusion as the likely source of their presenting issues, these clients can develop new skills in creating healthier boundaries in their relationships. This is usually a difficult step in the recovery process, and tests the therapeutic alliance. To move on, he or she must emancipate from the offending parent. Since this parent is usually unwilling to acknowledge the incestuous bond, and thus discourage this necessary separation, the client has the sole burden of initiating the "leave-taking." To many clients, the consequences, both real and imagined, often seem overwhelming. We need to be particularly aware of the pace and extent of the client's reactions to this step toward independence. It is wise to be conscious of sending positive messages of support, validation, and clinical availability to assist the client, as well as predicting and inoculating the client against the inevitable rejection and defensiveness on the part of the parent. We can assist the client in developing and practicing a repertoire of successful assertive strategies and boundary experiences before encouraging the client to confront the parent. These problem-solving skills and the confidence that all survivors of abuse need to develop is inherently a major portion of the therapeutic process. Empowering the client to identify and develop their own resources for continued recovery is the ultimate goal.

Survivors of covert abuse have learned to exist for the benefit of another (parent). For many survivors, it is common for them to transfer their inappropriate parent bond to another—including the therapist. Therefore the final therapeutic task in the treatment process is to provide the survivor an "arena" to gain skills encouragement and permission to emancipate, not only from the parent, but from the therapist as well.

SIBLING INCEST: "THE MYTH OF MUTUALITY"*

One is still challenged to unearth information on what may be one of the last taboos: sibling incest. Historically, society has tended to romanticize sexual activity between siblings. It is frequently dismissed as age-appropriate, mutually agreed-upon sexual exploration. Sibling incest has often been portrayed as non-damaging or less traumatic and treated as a minor, mild or even non-traumatic form of sexual abuse. The issues inherent in these family dynamics are frequently misunderstood in the overall therapeutic process. *Sibling incest* refers to sexual behavior between siblings of a more intimate nature than is usually included in normal child sexual development and experimentation. Incest between an older brother and a younger sister is the most commonly occurring type. In comparison to parent-child incest, little is known about sibling incest because reported cases are rare, since most parents who discover such incest activity are unlikely to "turn in" their child.

* Russell, D.E.H. 1986

Reporting is further complicated by the societal stigma that stipulates that males are "prohibited" from disclosing sexual abuse by older siblings who may be female because of the "macho" way men are socialized. The predominant view of sibling incest has been of mutual sexual exploration among children within the same age range. This is viewed as a normal occurrence in a child's psychosexual development.

The discrepancy in the severity of the aftereffects of sibling abuse typically have been attributed to age differential between the participants, the consent of the victim or the lack thereof, the age of victim at the time of the abuse, as well as the expressed or non-responsive reactions of the parents upon disclosure.

While sibling incest could result from a normal sexual curiosity, experimentation, or even sex play that's "gone too far"; it is more often due to situational pressures, personality disorders, dysfunction within the family system and/or the assumption of inappropriate roles within the family.

Both victim and offender may engage in these behaviors as an attempt to cope with unmet psychological needs such as the desire for affiliation and affection, combating loneliness, depression or isolation as well as an inappropriate discharging of anxiety and tension due to stressors.

The incest sometimes turns violent, which occurs in the rare instance when the offender acts out sexually with weaker siblings to gratify a need for retaliation, retribution, control or power. There are those mental health professionals, who believe that under certain specific circumstances, sibling incest may not be a traumatic, or even an unpleasant experience This approach is sensible only when applying it to the traditional "playing doctor" and is just another part of growing up, as both partners are sexually naive. (Forward and Buck, 1982) Other considerations to evaluate are:

- *If* the children are young and approximately the same age,
- *If* there is no betrayal or lack of trust between them,
- *If* the sexual play is the result of their natural curiosity and exploration
- *If* the children are not traumatized by disapproving adults who stumble upon them during the sex play.

However, there is evidence that where there were some positive feelings, or even ambivalence about the activities, the trauma response was often greater than when the experience was totally "unwanted." This contradicts the belief that sibling incest can be discounted as non-abusive or non harmful as it only involves "playing doctor"

Similar to the more frequently occurring parent-child abuse, survivors of sibling abuse report occurrences of lowered sexual self-esteem, depression and guilt surrounding the sexual activity, re-victimization experiences, suicide attempts, dissociative disorders and substance abuse. Prepubescent sibling incest can produce adjustment difficulties as participants begin dating, sexually interacting with peers, or becoming sex partners in a significant monogamous relationship.

When a woman's first sexual encounter/experience is with a sibling, in a coercive secret, possibly guilt-ridden atmosphere, this can left lasting imprints on her self-concept and development of normal sexual identity. Guilt and shame become identified responses with sexuality and can produce dysfunctions of varied severity.

Sibling incest experiences cannot be ignored. They need to be examined, explored and evaluated to determine if the presenting issues, problematic behaviors, and underlying concerns are influenced and impacted by these experiences. In providing treatment to survivors of sibling incest, the following relevant issues should be addressed:

1. **NORMAL SEXUAL BEHAVIOR**—It is important to evaluate and determine the client's perception of normalized sexual behavior looking at cultural, ethnic and geographic perspectives. Did they view what happened as victimization or acceptable interactions? Psycho-sexual and educational inquiries will allow the client to look at their interactions through different "glasses" to determine the underlying motivations and behaviors.

2. **AGE OF THE SIBLINGS**—This speaks to the age-appropriateness of interactions and when looking at age discrepancies, addressing the acceptable psycho-sexual behaviors. The issue that age is not the only determination of power differentials needs to be examined. In many cases, the mere fact that the older perpetrator is a brother is enough to give the perpetrator inherent power over the sister. In many cultures and societies, males are seen as traditionally holding power over females. Whether the sister is responsive to the social pressure of males over females or whether she sees power reflected and demon-

strated in her entire family hierarchy is of little significance. If she feels powerless or threatened, she might submit in order to "survive."

3. **NATURE & DURATION OF THE INCEST**—Was the sexual contact consistent with developmental levels of both participants (looking, exposing, fondling)? Or was it inappropriate and reflective of more advanced sexual knowledge and experiences (fellatio, sodomy or intercourse). Understanding the type of contact allows for the possibility of perpetrator's own victimization which is being mirrored by his acting out on his/her younger sibling.

4. **ACCESS TO THE VICTIM**—Was the contact *consensual?* Did both parties agree? Was there initial consent to exploration and sex play, but no further? *However*, even though a younger sibling agrees to her older sibling's invitation to "fool around," it does not mean that consent was given. Cooperation does not suggest that they fully understood the nature of the sexual interactions. Was the victim's naiveté exploited, or was the victim *enticed or seduced* by bribes or other means? Was the younger child *intimidated* by threats, aggressive verbal expressions, or even physical force to obtain the sexual contact?

5. **INTENT OF THE PARTICIPANTS**—In assessing the overall impact to the survivor, determine if the incest occurred as part of a broader interests and interactions between the parties. Were the interactions seen as *exploration* between the siblings? This occurs with the most regularity, and for many, is viewed as the least traumatic of the incidents of incest. The interaction between the siblings may not have been sexually motivated. If siblings are left alone for long periods of time due to family dynamics, and have unsupervised time together, incestuous interactions can occur. There are frequently inappropriate expectations placed by parents on older siblings; that they should be willing or able to care for their younger siblings in the parent's absence. In reality, the older child may be chronologically older, but not mature enough to act as a surrogate parent or caretaker. Dynamically, the parent(s) may be so caught up with their own life situations, that they are unable to effectively parent the children regarding appropriate interactions. As the children are left to their own devices, conduct can occur that is inappropriate or damaging. Parents who discover

the incest may not know how to put an end to the behavior, and as a result of their ineffective parenting skills, the abuse continues. There are also the cases where because of generational family dynamics, the parents believe that the abuse is "normal" and thus does not require their intervention. This is why it is important to gather as much generational family history as the client can offer. As the client describes the interactions with their sibling, it may be viewed that the incest was more an act of retaliation or retribution, where the abuser is attempting to get even for past injustices inflicted upon them, either real or imagined. The incest is used to degrade and humiliate the victim. The goal of the offender is to express anger. When this *retribution* intensifies and includes a level of *power and control* it brings with it an underlying intent to manipulate, overpower and control the victim. The use of intimidation and fear are most prevalent, particularly when the threat of harm is used to "keep the secret." Enforced secrecy is especially damaging to the survivor as it leads them to experience guilt and shame. They believe that they have to remain silent about what happened. Even worse, they often consider themselves to blame for what happened.

6. **FAMILY DYNAMICS**—In addition to the issues raised above, we may need to assist the client in gaining a greater understanding of the relationships and interactions within their families of origin that could have triggered the incest. Was there explicit or implicit acceptance of sexual behaviors? Was the father seen to favor "sexual freedom," allowing himself to walk around the house in a state of undress (or in his underwear)? Were there sexual explicit materials left in the open, for children to see and interpret? More recently in the advent of cable television, and the wide spectrum of sexually explicit television shows available, were these shows watched in the presence of children, thus affording them an ability to want to "act out" what they have seen? A more thorough exploration of all of these potentialities may allow the client to more effectively understand the underlying dynamics of their family.

7. **DISCLOSURES**—After disclosure, it was seen that many times, parents or other people in authority knew, witnessed or at least suspected the interactions. Many times victim disclosures are disregarded and followed-up with threats to allow the

abuse to continue. Many survivors of sibling abuse relate that the lack of parental responsibility (denial, complicity, failure to protect) was *more* traumatic than the effects of the actual sibling incest. Some female survivors relate pretending to be asleep when the sibling approached her, while others reported that at the time of the abuse they were too young to understand what was happening. Some kept the family secret because of implied or explicit threats. In many cases I (Mark) have treated, where the abuse occurred before the age of nine, none talked of fighting off, or denying the advances of their abusers because they believed that they were powerless to do so. Carrying the belief system of minding and obeying their parents, some survivors relate not disclosing the abuse to their parents, because it occurred during a time the older sibling was babysitting, and the victim had been told (by the parents) to obey the older sibling. All of the survivors spoke of self-blame and guilt. Many tell that the parents were non-responsive to hearing what the survivor attempted to communicate. There were repeated incidences where the parents blamed the victim and feeling re-victimized by her parents for their failure to intervene or protect her.

In examining some of the dynamics that cause siblings to abuse each other, the act of an older brother abusing his younger sister, typically involves some degree of one of the following variants:

A pubescent or adolescent brother uses his younger and usually naive sister for sexual experimentation. A socially inept and parentally neglected brother substitutes his sister for unavailable age-appropriate female peers of for lacking affection or nurturance. Clients also report that after exploring family dynamics, that their brother were themselves physically or sexually abused and this is their mechanism for dealing with their own anger, resentment and rage. Survivors of older brother younger sister abuse are less likely to marry than survivors of other incest experiences. They are more likely to be physically abused in their marriages if they marry. They are also more susceptible to unwanted sexual advances by an authority figure or other forms of sexual harassment. As children they were more fearful of sexual advances, and as adults they continue to remain fearful of being assaulted. Survivors need to be assisted in the therapeutic process to better understand and have validated these dynamics, so they can find more appropriate ways to deal with their anxiety and fears. Normalizing these reactions and concerns allows the client to acknowledge their history and begin to move beyond these events, in a constructive and more responsible manner.

In sister-initiated abuse of a younger sibling, usually brothers, seductiveness or tenderness may be demonstrated toward the younger child. She is likely to be insecure with peers or within the family and to use her brother for affection, security and reassurances. However, it is also possible that she may be quite aggressive, possessive, and demanding of her brother both sexually and in other ways. Understandably when these dynamics occur, the aftereffects are more profound. As previously stated, when a male victim feels they can't admit to the abuse, because of the society's perspective of "machismo" then the shame and regret are magnified. Boys that are abused by older siblings can feel that engaging in sexual activity with an older female is a form of "initiation" into manhood in spite of its negative effects. A feeling of pride may be mingled with any feelings of shame or guilt.

In situations where the abuse occurs with siblings of the same gender, especially if the children are under the age of ten, there should be no implicit belief that the behaviors imply homosexuality. When the molestation occurs between same sex adolescents siblings, there may be better indicators of homosexuality orientation. However, the homosexual preference of the initiator would generally *precede* the incest, rather than being its outcome. Such incest behaviors may lead to confusion on the part of the victim about their sexual identity.

This discussion of covert abuse and sibling incest, hopefully can serve the therapist as a guide in conducting a more comprehensive and assessment process. These types of incest are regularly not addressed. The client does not always identify some of the interactions discussed as abusive. With the therapist asking questions directed toward determining if these interactions occurred, and possibly offering explanations and clarity to what some of the behaviors could represent, it provides for clients' validation and acknowledgment for their history.

Abby, a 23-year-old woman, came to treatment requesting assistance in dealing with a series of unsuccessful relationships. She reported that her last significant relationship ended when her boyfriend accused her of being "sexually frigid." She continued to describe a series of interactions that repeatedly ended when the men alluded to her unavailability. During the assessment, Abby was asked if she had ever been exposed to any traumas in her life, including sexual ones. When the question was posed, Abby took a reflective long pause, and then stated "I don't think so, but let me think about it and I'll get back to you.

The following session, Abby asked the clinician, "What exactly did you mean by sexual trauma?" The therapist explained some of the dynamics and indicators of incest and trauma, and asked Abby "Do you think any of these situations or behaviors may be relevant to you?" Again a reflective pause and a response "I don't think so, but let me think about it."

With a deliberate attempt to avoid influencing her thinking, the issue of "incest" was not raised again by the therapist. The next several sessions involved problem-solving, solution-focused ideas to help Abby continue to evaluate how her current behaviors influence her relationships. After the sixth session, Abby returned for treatment. As the session began, with no prompting, the following exchange took place:

Abby: You remember that question you asked about sex and possible trauma?

Mark: Of course.

Abby: Do you think it's abusive when your brother gets into the shower with you without asking, and begins washing you in places he really shouldn't?

Mark: What do you think?

Abby: Well, until you asked the question, I really had never thought about it. But now you got me thinking, I seem to remember that it made me feel uncomfortable.

Abby: I remember thinking that this shouldn't be happening, but also knowing my parents, and how they saw my brother, they'd never believe he would do this.

Mark: So they would have thought you made it up?

Abby: Probably, but them not believing me about other things probably wouldn't have helped the situation.

Mark: So you never told anyone before now?

Abby: One time I mentioned it to my brother, but he blew me off and said it was no big deal. He also made it clear that no one would believe me, and hinted that if I told, there would be trouble, so I just kept quiet. He came in a few more times, but then he

seemed to lose interest, so it just stopped. Even though it both-
ered me, I never thought it was a big deal.

Mark: How do you feel about it now as we speak about it?

Abby: I don't really think much about it. Can something like that really
have some effect on me eight years afterwards?

Mark: I guess it has since we are now talking about it and how you feel
eight years after it happened.

Treatment with Abby progressed and the issues involving her
understanding and acceptance of the interactions with her brother
became clearer. She continued to get in touch with previously undefined reactions regarding the abuse by her brother. As the work
evolved, her feeling and confusion regarding own sexuality and how
she had allowed it to unconsciously impact her current relationships
abated to the degree that, permitted Abby to invest greater energy in
maintaining safer boundaries and integrity with other people, particularly men. The psycho-sexual "education" that Abby was able to utilize, occurred because the therapist asked the question, that might
have been omitted without a better perspective on the different and
under-reported aspects of sibling incest and sexual molestation.

Concluding this chapter, we cannot forget that sexual abuse
inside the family is often easier to keep hidden, particularly when
family members conspire to cover up and discredit the victim or
when it is so subtle, that the effects are insidious and unconscious.

[10]

Diagnostic Errors and Oversights

For every complex question, there is usually a simple answer. And it's usually wrong.

—H. L. Menken.

One of the most challenging aspects of the counseling and psychotherapy field today is determining an appropriate assessment of our client's presenting issues and potential underlying problems. In the best of all possible worlds, we would help the clients to set and reach their own therapeutic goals regardless of the mandate for the standardized "assessment" tool called a diagnosis. We must face the hard reality that we have to come up with some type of diagnosis for symptoms and an evaluation of a 'mental disorder' to satisfy the requirements of HMOs or reimbursable insurance vouchers. In this chapter, we will clarify the common diagnostic mistakes that can be made as many of the emotional and behavioral symptoms manifested by survivors mimic those of other categories. In describing salient components of both post-traumatic stress disorder as well as borderline personality disorder, we can demonstrate how easy it is to get sidetracked or confused.

NORMALIZING THE "LABEL"

Many adult victims of sexual abuse have survived the abuse only to suffer the more insidious disability of being labeled with a mental disorder because of their complaints and the specific symptoms presented. It is insidious as those labels follow us long after the initial reality of the incestuous or abusive experience supposedly has

133

been resolved. As they suffer long-term losses of self-esteem, positive motivation and an increase in the intensity and frequency of negative self-talk, they often believe the reality of the disorder label, and apply it to themselves as "truth" in determining their personal identity.

What do we do when the complex of complaints described by the client and the symptomology displayed overlap the descriptors of various diagnostic categories of the DSM-IV? We may wonder what kind of diagnosis we should give to clients who complain about having difficulty with otherwise stable relationships, feel less than whole, and who actively disparage the many different therapists they have consulted, apparently receiving no improvement in their complaints. They may describe vague or specific memories that have become intrusive to their everyday living and cause them physical or emotional distress. When we add issues of low self-esteem and self-worth, instability of mood, as well as bouts of excessive depression, the clarity of the situation becomes even more muddled.

In the course of the therapy, we may recognize signals that our clients have become manipulative, confrontational or even suicidal. We might think it is easy to justify the all too familiar diagnosis of "borderline personality disorder"—based on how *this* client makes us feel and our internal responses to her. The frequent emotional outbreaks and inappropriate abreactions to seemingly normal events that cause undue stress may reinforce this perception. One of the problems of working with a borderline is that at first they seem so 'normal.' She usually holds down a job that she does appropriately, if not competently. She might even tell us she's benefiting from our work together. We begin to believe that we can "make a difference." We know that metaphorically, borderlines walk a tightrope between sanity and madness. They are generally unable to form consistent, long-term, intimate relationships as well as being incapable of achieving insight into their personal problems. Borderline clients seem to be constantly struggling to break free from an underlying corrosive sense of worthlessness and rage that frequently spill over into self-destructive behaviors and consequences. They are chronically depressed, purposefully addicted, compulsively divorced, and seemingly living from one emotional crisis or disaster to another.

Craving intimacy, borderlines reject it. They gravitate towards impulsive, impetuous and unpredictable behavior patterns that result in unworkable social liaisons. Often going unsuccessfully from therapist to therapist, a properly diagnosed borderline hopes to find a magic pill for those overwhelming feelings of emptiness, insomnia, panic and generalized anxiety. This group of clients makes up the main core of a "dual diagnosis" paradigm, turning to chemicals and alcohol looking for a respite from this intense internal turmoil. They may leave a hospital stay looking good, raising their own hopes as well as those in their world—until the next crisis (real or imagined) or the next excursion into self-damage. All of these disturbances in areas of affect regulation, impulse control, reality testing, interpersonal relationships and self-integration make the treatment a proverbial "land mine of volatility" as the therapist attempts to maintain a relationship, while the client is doing their best to test the system.

When we attempt to identify a therapeutic issue to focus on based on their complaints, they may get into a defensive mode, deny the problem and/or get angry that "we don't understand them." *What they don't do is change*, and then we are left to wonder why. The more we know about borderline personalities reinforces our belief that they never get better despite all our good efforts. We may apply this label to these "difficult" clients because they question our competence and sensibilities. Therefore, we run the risk of getting confused by the implications of the label, and because we "know" they can't get better, we give up on helping our clients.

Ascribing the label of this personality disorder to our client does not accurately provide an understanding of the symptoms in specific relationship to a client's psycho-social history, expectations and goals for themselves. This lack of comprehension makes it more difficult for corrective therapeutic change to occur. In fact, it distracts us from considering and applying a more useful diagnosis. The application of a model of treatment that focuses on the sexual abuse offers a way to integrate the trauma and to prevent further symptom formation and recurrence. The manipulative behaviors and other symptoms that can cause the label are more appropriately viewed in the context of *"learned survival responses"* that were once adaptive and appeared reasonable, but no longer are appropriate in the client's current environment.

A more helpful approach is to ask yourself a question. *"How is it possible in the world for any person to develop such a negative outlook on life which generates self-destructive behaviors and attitudes?"* The thoughts in response to this question will lead to inquiring about events in their history which could explain how badly they feel about themselves.

In a study conducted by Saxe, Van der Kolk, Beckowitz, Chinman, Hall, et al (1993), and detailed in the American Journal of

Psychiatry, 150 (7), 1037–1042, 100% of 110 psychiatric inpatients, who were previously diagnosed with schizophrenia, mood disorders, and borderline personality disorder, were in fact, individuals with dissociative disorders. (Bell-Gadsby & Siegenberg, 1996)

> Many of the difficulties associated with treating border-
> lines might be alleviated by providing a therapy which
> focuses on the trauma. (Courtois, 1988, page 161)

John Briere (1986) states,

> Current treatment approaches to Borderline Personality
> Disorders stress theoretical formulations which are rela-
> tively devoid of reference to sexual victimization (e.g. object
> relations theory). It is quite possible that treatment that
> directly deals with the abuse will be more successful with
> such clients.

It is also true that survivors of sexual abuse display the same pattern of symptoms and complaints as do borderlines. They have not learned effective coping strategies and skills that could change these internal knee-jerk responses. Based on their prior interactions, including their abuse experiences, they have learned that you can't trust many people. This lack of validation from potent and influential 'others' in our client's personal history and environment often generates an intense sense of self-doubt and recrimination. Fearing these feelings, this class of clients creates interpersonal distance to prevent themselves from being hurt again. They will do anything to avoid re-experiencing any hint of a stimulus that may further associate them with their trauma. This includes the occasional impulsive decision to discontinue therapy. To rationalize this decision, they may characterize the discomfort experienced in therapy as evidence of abuse which has not stopped, and consider the therapist as a new form of abuser.

It is our contention that "post-traumatic stress disorder" (PTSD) is much more appropriate a diagnosis than that of "borderline" for many of our clients. The after-effects of living through traumatic events like incest or sexual molestation will clearly make one distrustful of the integrity of people who should have been caretakers and protectors. It is very plausible that the distrust would generalize to other intimates. Without repeating the complaints and behaviors mentioned above, it is evident that the effects of surviving such ego-damaging experiences will last until the reality of the abuse is addressed and interventions made. A colleague once told me (Mark) as I struggled to help a client who I was *sure* had to be a Borderline, that I had to be careful to "not get afflicted with that dreaded disease, '*hardening of the categories.*'" He was trying to tell me that just because this person is presenting all the symptoms and behaviors of the borderline; it does not necessarily define their identity.

We can recognize that just because a client is difficult doesn't automatically make them a borderline personality. As we take their psychosocial history, it is easy to look for a rational basis and a behavioral explanation for their responses of reluctance, fear, apprehension and their apparent attempts to elicit non-caring responses from others. They seem compelled to respond to the discomfort of coming to grips with their abuse in an acceptable way. This drive to reduce personal discomfort can interpret or transform the actions or words of an otherwise empathic clinician into just another example of an uncaring individual in her mind. They often exhibit a disguised presentation of themselves, which generates an overlapping between different diagnostic categories. This possible confusion is something that we must all be cognizant of when deciding the appropriate treatment course for any of our clients.

> Sally came to treatment complaining that for the last several years she has had a prevailing sense of doom and gloom. By her own estimation she was "under-employed," working in a job where her true "talents" we not being used. Her long-term relationship with her boyfriend was going nowhere. She mentioned that she had developed a belief that people only evaluated her by her outward appearance: a rather obese, spike-haired, heavily made-up woman whose mode of dress seemed to accentuate the "large" parts of her body. She also believed that people were negatively judgmental about her tattoos, which were prominently displayed on her ankles and just above her breast area.
>
> As an aside, she mentioned *"Oh, and by the way, I've been a prescription drug abuser for the last ten years. All attempts at rehab have failed. My last therapist fired me because I would not comply with his request to admit myself to the hospital. No one can tell me I can't do this by myself."*
>
> Sally proceeded to talk about her rather chaotic and violent family of origin. Her father physically abused her mother and sexually fondled both her and her sisters. Her mother, Jane, had been told about the fondling on numerous occasions, but told Sally that she (Jane) would not consider leaving because she

couldn't "afford" to lose her husband and the financial support he provided. Eventually the physical abuse became so severe that indeed Jane was forced to end the marriage. Sally and her mother struggled for years to develop an appropriate, warm relationship, even attending dyad counseling with three separate therapists over a six year period. Sally reports her mother didn't like any of the therapists because, *"Each of them sided with me."* (Sally) in criticizing Jane for not protecting her.

As our work together began to address her interpersonal relationship issues, Sally became increasingly less reliable in her attendance. These included multiple sexual encounters, three terminated pregnancies, and a current relationship with a married boyfriend who would see her whenever he could "slip away," and would suddenly appear in her bed in the middle of the night, wearing ". . . nothing more than a smile." This affair had been continuing for three years, with the man declaring a desire to leave his wife, but always finding a reason he couldn't do it right now. Sally was beginning to believe he would never follow up on his promise, but had no clue as to how she could make him change his mind or how to handle her intense disappointment.

The issues and feeling revolved around her incestuous encounters with her father were areas of conversation that brought the greatest emotional response from Sally. I framed her symptoms as those which typically and frequently result from such sexual abuse. Although she was able to talk about feeling betrayed and victimized, the vulnerable feelings were quickly masked and glossed over with irrelevant comments such as whether she should take her car in for service this week or next. Any attempt to redirect her back to the painful memories of her childhood were met with comments related to how I (Mark) must enjoy "torturing me" and all the others like her.

As a demonstration of how uncomfortable Sally was with the discussion of her abuse, she would "distract" the conversation with talk of some incident in her life that she wanted to better understand. These issues seemed to always involve interactions with others that showed her in a bad light, and ended with a relationship ending, or with her being left alone. These stories were ways that Sally could effectively keep me at arms distance and prevent me from getting to the underlying concerns relevant to her abuse. Her best defense was a repeated attempt to make me devalue her and her life choices. Each session would involve a story that presented her pre-conceived notion that she was unable to have positive, honest relationships with people, including her therapist. Consequently, this excuse allowed her to blame this "disability" and any other current crisis for her abuse of prescription drugs.

If I attempted to refocus some of her concerns to a better awareness of the significance of her abuse, Sally would deflect discussions of feeling responses by exploiting the substance abuse issue. On more than a handful of occasions she would report to me that "After our last visit I had a real urge to abuse (drugs), but I didn't. Aren't you proud?" When I didn't express my "pride" demonstratively enough to reward her abstinence, Sally would become annoyed or hurt. She began missing appointments, stating that I had not written them down for her. After missing two appointments in a row, she asked whether it was still okay for her to return to treatment. The urge to "rid" myself of a difficult non-compliant client was strong. On the other hand, I believed that Sally's behaviors were more symbolic of her long-standing, ineffective coping mechanism that in the context of her maladaptive survival skills made her resistance easier to relate with therapeutically. I was not willing to allow her behaviors either in or out of the therapy room to precipitate what seemed to be her 'desired' outcome: someone else rejecting or abandoning her because of who she was or how she behaved. Terminating prematurely with Sally would have been in conflict with what seemed to me to be important considerations for Sally; her current inadequate understanding of how to better get her needs met, without drugs or engaging in destructive relationships.

At the time, Sally believed that her survival was preserved and protected by not allowing anyone to get too close, so she would not be hurt. When she did let her defenses down, and felt the resulting intra-psychic pain or rejection, she would medicate it, and forget it. Her anxiety about revealing herself in therapy was greater than she could handle, and with increasing frequency, she admitted that her prescription drug use had resumed. She would make attempts to cut back, but with minimal success. It became clear that drug intervention now superceded therapeutic work regarding her incest history. Once again, Sally was adamant in her refusal to seek inpatient care, stating she would be placing her job at risk if they found out "I was using again." She would repeatedly commit to investigating alternative treatment plans for her drug use, but would not follow through.

With each failure to follow through on a recommendation from me regarding drug detoxification or treatment, Sally would present a nonverbal "ultimatum" focusing on whether or not I would "fire" her from treatment like her last therapist did. I didn't react in the way she had expected. Instead, I told her that I understood her ambivalence about dealing with her drug addiction, and how it allows her to medicate her unhappy feelings. Sally escalated by becoming even more non-compliant with her treatment tasks.

Her usage began to have a more primary effect on her daily living and the need for intensive drug treatment became a fevered topic of discussion. After missing or canceling a number of appointments, Sally called to inform me that she was making arrangement to get treatment for her drugs and "I'll be in touch."

Four months passed with no contact. Sally then called me to ask for a new appointment. As expected, she had not sought out any drug treatment program. As her rationale, she argued that the timing was not right. I still believe that her continued drug use was a roadblock to her being able to therapeutically deal with her abuse history. I told Sally my feelings, but left open the possibility that she could return for treatment after she addressed her drug issues. I told her that with a decided effort to deal with her history, she could begin to reclaim herself esteem and self worth.

Idealistic as it may seem, my hope for Sally is that at some future point, once she gets control over her drug use, she may be able to integrate the insight and information we processed and be ready to face the effects of her trauma directly. Until that time, it is reasonable to predict that Sally will continue to struggle with these issues. Right now, she believes that masking her 'doom and gloom' outlook in drug use is her best alternative.

I do not view this as a treatment failure. I use this example of a client who if I had misdiagnosed her as simply Borderline would not have been offered the opportunity to at least discuss her abusive history in the context of her current behaviors and lifestyle. I do hope that Sally will eventually seek out further clinical intervention, and I believe that on some level of cognizance she was able to incorporate parts of the work we did together, and it will help that process get a better start toward her eventual recovery from sexual abuse.

Clearly, I look back and wonder if I could have found a better way to address her many needs. However, I am also aware that her history and resultant personality characteristics generated her many difficulties with interpersonal relationships and self-integration. These precluded her ability to develop a therapeutic alliance. Somehow developing a sense of safety in the therapy room as she discussed her history was not sufficient. However, I also believe that by giving Sally some understanding of how she "uses" her drug addiction to mask her underlying feelings, valued and gave credence her current behaviors, although they could have easily been viewed in the context of "she'll never get better." This would fit the preconceived notion frequently held when someone with many of Sally's personality traits and behaviors presents for treatment, and we quickly label them Borderline Personality because she was resistant to the work we are presenting, and was constantly testing the limits of the relationship.

FALSE MEMORY ACCUSATIONS

One of the confounding issues confronting those of us working with survivors is the belief of some people, particularly client's family members or perpetrators, that clinicians "help" the client remember abusive or incestuous events in the past that really didn't occur. This theory implies an "evil" intention on the part of the therapist, who at the worst, would ally with an angry and vindictive client to wreak havoc on their parent's lives with these false allegations; or on the other end of the "conspiracy" spectrum, would influence a vulnerable, naïve client, which would lead to the need for a lengthy treatment course.

The notion of "False Memory," that has focused the media's attention to False Memory Syndrome and its like-named Foundation, has had a tremendous impact on how, and sometimes if, clinicians were willing to work with these survivors. A newly acknowledged, yet controversial, emphasis on the issues relevant to memory and whether or not recovered memories could be considered valid memories, gained acceptance as the False Memory Syndrome Foundation brought their perspective, supported by certain psychiatrist and other mental health professionals, into the public awareness. This group supported the belief that repressed memory was a fallacy, and that had past traumatic incidents occurred, the current memory(s) one had of the experience, would be clear and specific in its context. This belief, promoted by self-anointed false memory "experts," only succeeded in devaluing or discrediting survivors who had in their adult life spontaneously recalled childhood experiences that were viewed as traumatic to them.

For many years, there has been the belief that clinicians were vulnerable to accusations of unethical behaviors because they were working with a client who recovered specific memories of past traumas during the course of treatment. These memories had been blocked from full or partial emergence to the conscious mind since childhood, possibly due to the an undefined sort of protective 'armor' or shielding that the person used as they were not yet ready to deal with her past abusive experiences.

The False Memory Syndrome Foundation has also stirred the flames of another controversy, the undermining of the therapist role with survivors of sexual abuse. Some therapists have been sued by parents of adult children molested by them, as these parents wrap themselves in a heavy veil of self-righteousness, vigorously defending their honor and ensconcing themselves in a state of denial that nothing ever happened. Some of the most well-known clinicians working in this field have had their livelihoods threatened by families, and perpetrators, who have taken them to court to protest an adult's recollection or recovery of childhood memories of their abuse. These "nay-sayers" offer their belief that children cannot with any degree of accuracy, remember the abuse, particularly if it occurred a decade or two ago. Therefore, it *must* be the clinician brainwashing, or corrupting the client to come up with these memories.

It is well documented that subjects witnessing the same scenario report different observations that are products of their personal interest filters. After time has passed, the memories are even more varied and distorted. Because of this very fluid nature of both good and bad memories, many different thoughts about events that have occurred in our lives are responsive to suggestion. When we talk with our clients, particularly using a solution-focused model, we may suggest potential *positive* outcomes. This does not imply making suggestions about the initiation or causality of the problems. There is a broad line between suggestion and corruption. Clients are encouraged to remember, but are not forced to do so. There is no question but that both accusers and accused are vehement in their beliefs. There is no objective process available to know who is right. As we work with this population, we must be aware and distinguish the contexts of the work. It is an entirely different matter, and much more acceptable, to treat those clients who have known all along that they were abused. They come to therapy to discuss and heal from that acknowledged abuse. The silver lining to the False Memory Syndrome cloud is that it is forcing therapists to reexamine with a critical eye the way they practice, in order to determine how ethical it truly is. It is therefore a prudent and ethical practice to go at the client's pace, and if there is traumatic memory, it will eventually bubble in the conscious mind when the client is ready to reintegrate the memory in a way that is meaningful and healing for her. (Bell-Gadsby & Siegenberg, p. 7)

When we meet our clients and listen to their stories, we must be aware that the mere presence of symptoms is not evidence of abuse. If you were to peruse any checklist of symptoms resulting from sexual abuse, you will find they are so general, that anyone can fit into one or more of those categories. When we look at the pattern of symptoms, we can only project what they mean. The problem with the advice, guidance and suggestions that the therapist offers is that we can *create* victims based on an uncritical acceptance of false premises of trauma and memory.

Therapists offer simple answers to hard questions. It is like the old story of "fish in the dreams." The story concerns a well-known "analytical" psychiatrist who attributed all patient problems to the presence of 'fish in the dreams.' A patient consults him, tells his story, and the psychiatrist begins to question him about the presence of fish in his dreams. When the patient informs him he has not dreamt of fish, the psychiatrist informed him that of course, his "unconscious" would be holding back this memory from his conscious awareness. He must go back and relate his last dream. Wishing to be cooperative, the patient recalled that he dreamed about going out to dinner.

> *"Wonderful!"* the psychiatrist replied, *"Does the restaurant ever serve fish?"*
>
> "I suppose it does."
>
> *"And does it ever rain around that restaurant?"*
>
> "Well, sure—but . . ."
>
> *"When it rains, do puddles form in the street?"*
>
> "Yes, it does."
>
> *"Isn't it possible that fish can be tossed out of the restaurant and can live in those puddles?"*

"Why I guess so."

"Voila, I was right again—fish in your dreams!"

There is always an inherent risk in blurring the line between probing for information and creating it. Is it digging or undue persuasion? As we listen to the client's story, the level and intensity of the details of their memories do not necessarily make a memory more accurate. We have to remember that manufactured memories caused by whatever reason are usually indistinguishable from real ones unless there is substantiated external evidence. Beliefs precede memories. Michael Yapko, in an article in the Family Therapy Networker Magazine (September-October, 1993) tells of a distraught client who comes to see him because his adult daughter has just confronted him with horrific allegations of child sexual abuse. This gentleman could not fathom why a daughter with whom he always believed that he had a caring, close, nurturing relationship could accuse him of such behaviors. Only after further discussion was it revealed that his daughter had been "helped" to uncover these memories while in therapy. She had entered treatment to gain greater insight into why she was having difficulty making and sustaining relationships. After the therapist had heard the woman talk generally about feelings of sadness, guilt, insecurity and inadequacies, the therapist announced at the end of the very first hour, that she knew the underlying cause of the client's difficult: she had been sexually abused. The client was adamant in her denial that she had no memory of ever having been abused. She stated she had a loving, caring relationship with her father. The therapist's response was, "Don't worry. *It* (the memory of the abuse) will come." The client continued to deny that any problem had existed, and insisted that she was happy with her relationship with her father. Each time this therapist repeated, "Don't worry. 'It' will come." The therapist then suggested that she be hypnotized so that she could "get beneath" the conscious defenses which "obviously" prevented her from recalling the events. As the therapist had predicted, or more accurately, *suggested*, indeed the client eventually created memories which would fit the expectations of the therapist who had been warm, comforting and supportive. It is likely that this acceptance was conditional to the client's willingness in meeting the therapist's preconceived evaluation and appraisal of the situation. The woman confronted her father with her newfound beliefs and accusations as to what had occurred. Needless to say the father was appalled at his daughter's declarations and had consulted Dr. Yapko as to how to proceed.

After a period of time, the father was able to spend appropriate time with his daughter to discuss her allegations. The daughter consulted a neutral third party, different from either her therapist or the father's representative, and was helped to recognize the 'implanting' of 'false memories' by the suggestions of her therapist. She was able to objectively re-evaluate her accusations, and to revise the accompanying internal belief system regarding her father's actions. Although it did take some time to occur, a positive reconnection with her parents was accomplished.

This story had a happier ending than many, and only serves to illustrate the urgent need for therapist to allow clients an opportunity to recover their "own" memories. We don't need to "help" our client's remember their past histories. With our appreciation of the validity of their stories, we simply allow them the permission to construct or re-construct, (if necessary), their *own* realities. We can encourage them to view the world through their eyes, as cloudy as they may be, until the fog clears, and their image is better defined. The way we allow the process of collaboration to form the outcome speaks to the beauty of the resolution. As a farmer in Kansas once said, "Build it, and they will come." It is important to develop a collaborative therapeutic alliance that will permit the recovery of memories in a supportive, accepting manner that accepts, validates, and acknowledges the client's reality

It is an equally grievous error to attribute sexual abuse as a cause of every maladaptive behavior. Not every weight gain or relationship complaint has roots in sexual molestation. On the one hand, we want to be attuned to the possibility that such an event might have occurred, and gently inquire into the subject. On the other hand, we cannot afford the one-sided luxury of jumping on the abuse bandwagon and closing off other diagnostic or historical considerations.

CONCLUDING THOUGHTS AND COMMENTS

In the contents of this book, we have attempted to articulate a need to become more collaborative and attentive to the individual and unique needs of clients who have sought our help to deal with their many complex issues. When any client comes in for treatment, we rarely know if there has been a history of abuse. However, we must have within our theoretical framework an understanding and belief that clients who feel accepted and validated for any part of their history, are more likely to feel safe disclosing some of their most intrusive and traumatic experiences. Even as we hear these stories, we must take proper precautions to avoid a secondary trauma and therapist burnout as well as guarding against our personal feelings which may be stimulated by countertransference. As we get to know our client, we explore the negative belief systems and cognitive distortions which affect self-esteem and limit the client's capacity to meet their own expectations. By using an Ericksonian and NLP frame of reference in working with this patient population, we can focus our energy on being flexible, utilizing everything that the client brings in to the session, as well as formulating creative methods to treat this very unique individual. The model of shared collaboration that we use helps us work strategically with this particular client population, although many others could be beneficiaries of this type of approach. In forging this working alliance, we establish safety, security and a sense of trust that allows these very vulnerable survivors to reveal sensitive narratives in their history.

There are several concepts and methods derived from the Ericksonian treatment concepts to help transform the negative assumptions and limiting beliefs that have molded ineffective or often dysfunctional behavioral styles. An important element is to facilitate the healing of the wounded "inner child," and integrating that restored aspect of the ego into the functional adult.

To avoid dependency on the therapeutic relationship, planning for termination of therapy sessions is essential. It also must be done in a way that alleviates the fear of abandonment since the latter often results from the betrayal of trust.

There are two issues which need particular notice, although the treatment interventions could be the same. Covert abuse is the perpetrator's subtle manipulation of the client with sexual overtones which emotionally cripples its victim. Sibling incest or abuse is of special concern because it tends to be ignored or minimized by families who often protect the perpetrators and criticize a complaining victim. These forms of sexual abuse are well hidden whether due to shame, pressure by families to maintain the 'secrets,' or by simply adapting to the resulting double binds by pushing the bad memories into the recesses of the mind where it can fester. The multiple symptoms and complaints which result are often complicated by alcoholism and substance abuse, which can become diagnostic nightmares.

While we can guard against making suggestions of sexual abuse to vulnerable clients who will cling to any descriptive explanation of their symptoms from 'the experts,' we can remain curious and open to all the information with which we are presented so we do not ignore the signals. Our very framework of collaboration which established connection and trust allows the disclosure of the history. The very defensiveness of both perpetrators and families continue to deny validation of victims and sometimes becomes the seeds of reverse accusations of false memory. We are well advised to plan the therapy strategies purposefully and with care.

This book has attempted to offer our mutual visions of therapeutic collaboration for designing healing strategies which provide an opportunity for these abused clients to share their stories in an empowering and validating context, and make life-enhancing choices.

In addition to adding these treatment ideas to one's repertoire, we invite clinicians will use the information as a springboard to examine the assumptions that guide the philosophical and practical treatment approaches to working with victims of incest and sexual abuse. As we watch these survivors develop skills of self-nurturing and cognitive restructuring of negative belief systems, we can feel fulfilled by making a positive difference for people who have had their sense of trust and security stripped away. As you work with each unique client, relish the opportunity to use your creativity to design and develop your own positive healing strategies and techniques based on their stories and the collaborative framework in which clients participate to help themselves heal, opening up the world of "possibilities."

Appendix A

"VISUAL-KINESTHETIC DISSOCIATION"[1]

ADAPTED FROM RICHARD BANDLER

1. Make sure clients are comfortably "anchored" into familiar states of competence or security in the present. Use the associational cue or anchor of safety, comfort and security explained above, or the symbol, memory or place of safety that the client picked out during the first therapy session. This anchor is maintained during the entire therapeutic intervention.

2. Separate the visual memories of the abuse from the emotional reaction by inviting the client to imagine sitting in a "movie theater of the mind" and to throw the 'flashback' images up on an imaginary screen in her mind's eye. Instruct her to wash the color out of these images so that the images are black and white. This provides immediate edges and boundaries to the experience by virtue of the screen. Making it black and white helps to maintain distance and objectivity allowing our client to view the events without emotionality, as if it were happening to someone else at another time.

3. Ask the client to imagine that her cognitive faculties which are objective and non-emotional can drift up into a projection booth or can stand up behind her chair as she sits in the room feeling that safety and security. A useful metaphor for this objectivity is 'Sergeant Friday' ("Just the facts, Ma'am") from the TV series, Dragnet or 'Mr. Spock' or 'Data' for Star Trek fans. The

---

1 Bandler, Richard, *Using Your Brain—for a Change.* Moab, Utah: Real People Press, 1985.

client can use this objective perspective to learn something new by viewing the events without emotional biases.

4. Run this black-and-white "movie" of the traumatic events in 'fast' time beginning before the trauma and ending after the client is safe again. Unless the abuse is continuing, it did come to an end. This accomplishes three important tasks. Moving the images faster interrupts the habitual pattern in which they experience flashbacks, opening the mind to change. Since the client is in control of speed, color, focus and distance of the images, feelings of helplessness diminish. The intensity of the emotional response diminishes with the increased dissociation and resulting objectivity.

5. We invite our clients to use this objectivity to obtain and process logical information about those traumatic events that had been unavailable previously. The new information they have accumulated from this different perspective will relieve some 'guilt' or the 'woulda, coulda, shoulda' mentality. We can help survivors recognize and appreciate that indeed they did survive; never again will this crime happen to them in that same way; they did the best they could with the resources that they had at the time, and it was not their fault.

6. The client of the present, enhanced by this objectivity and information can internally comfort and validate the younger self who had experienced the assault and/or abuse. The essence of healing is self-comfort, logical and factual understanding and validation.

A PERSONAL STATE OF CALM/COMPETENCE[2]

1. Recall or create a personal experience or memory of security, calmness or competence. It can be from recent or long standing experience or drawn from imagining such an experience.

2. Associate or step into this imagined or remembered experience.

3. Describe your internal images, dialogue and physical sensations that accompany that resourceful state.

4. Connect that state to both a deep "satisfying" breath and to a word or phrase to anchor this resource physiologically and

---

2 Adapted from: Connirae Andreas and Steve Andreas, *Change Your Mind—and Keep the Change.* (Moab, Utah: Real People Press, 1987)

verbally. Rehearse this association until client can access it herself equally intensely.

5. Apply it to a recalled situation in which you feel less than comfortable and competent. As it integrates inside and changes your internal state, notice the difference.

EXTERNALLY ORIENTED SELF-HYPNOSIS[3]

1. Find a comfortable position for your body and a pleasant place to focus your eyes, knowing that throughout this experience, you can feel free to make any physical adjustments necessary to maintain your state of comfort and ease.

2. You can keep your eyes open or you may choose to close them, but do not do so until you feel comfortable enough to do that. Make sure you stay in the here and now.

3. If you want to reorient at any time, you can do this very easily just by moving around a bit. Another nice way would be to count to yourself from one to five, reminding yourself that you will be progressively more awake, alert and refreshed with each number.

4. Name aloud *five* (5) each sights, sounds and physical sensations you are aware of right now. Now name *four* (4) different examples of each, progressing downward until there is *one* (1) of each category.

5. Note that losing track of the requested numbers or categories is common, and is a sign that you are succeeding in accessing unconscious resources.

6. You can stop, and enjoy the comfort and peace of relaxing, free of having to think of anything. You may choose to repeat the process, either aloud or silently to deepen your experience.

7. You can use this opportunity to suggest positive suggestions or affirmations for yourself, and enjoy it thoroughly.

8. When you are ready, count up from one to five, moving your fingers, feet, arms and hands and head sequentially, suggesting progressive alertness, energy, and comfort with each number.

---

3 Adapted from: Dolan, Yvonne, *Resolving Sexual Abuse: Solution-Focused Therapy and Ericksonian Hypnosis for Adult Survivors,* Chicago: W.W. Norton, 1991.

Appendix B

SELF-ASSESSMENT QUESTIONS

- What type of clients will you *not* work with?
- How do you decide if a client is too difficult?
- Do you have a personal sense of your own limitations in working with clients?
- Do you extend your availability to your clients, by being accessible 24 hours a day, and thus deprive yourself of private time?
- Do you work weekends and /or holidays?
- Do you take vacations, and if so, will you deny your relaxation by accepting client calls?
- How many client-hours do you work per week?
- With how many clients are you comfortable?
- Are you willing to extend the limit for a client in crisis?
- Do you start and end sessions on time, or extend/expand session time during periods of abreactive work?
- How much of your personal feelings do you share in a session, in the moment?
- How much of your personal life do you share in a session, and for what reason?
- How do you identify the limits of your competency?
- Do you trust your intuition?
- How can you tell if you are within your comfort level?
- What is your comfort level with a client's story, especially when there is intense affect and content?

- What is your comfort level in experiencing "undefined process," while failing to understand much of what is happening in the moment?
- How long will you be willing to "stay with" a client who is "stuck"?
- Are you comfortable saying "NO"?
- Do you have structured time to unload confusion or frustration with colleagues?
- Do you receive regular supervision and/or consultation, and if appropriate, personal therapy?
- Do you find yourself talking about work with family or in social situations?
- Do you avoid talking about it at all?

Appendix C

SOLUTION-FOCUSED QUESTIONS

Solution-focused assessment questions will help focus on desired outcomes and will shift the therapeutic perspective into one of objectivity:

1. What happened that gave you the idea that therapy would be helpful, or would be the best place to sort out your difficulties?
2. If you've experienced a similar difficulty before, how did you deal with it? What about the times when the difficulty started to develop, but you stopped it before it went too far? (If they don't report any positive coping experiences, you can point out that *"You can't remember any time like that <u>right now</u>."*)
3. What are the things (activities, work, hobbies, relationships etc.) in your life right now that you would like to continue? If the client is asked to write a list of the above, this list can function later as a tangible symbol for the safety of the present. Some of these items on the list may also serve as associational cues for comfort and safety when other experiences may not come to mind.
4. How will you know when treatment is complete?
5. What will be the first or smallest signs that things are getting better? (Let them struggle with this if necessary.)
6. What will be the first sign of resolution that *others will notice* when you start to feel better?
7. What will you *do differently* when this trauma is less of a current problem in your life? How will you use your time differently?
8. What positive, useful things will you say to yourself? How will you think differently about the future?

9. Are there times when the above is already happening even to a small extent?

10. What differences will the above healing changes make when they have been present in your life over an extended period of time (days, weeks, months or years)?

Appendix D

RE-IMPRINTING*

ADAPTED FROM ROBERT DILTS

1. Ask the client to project a movie of that experience on an imaginary screen about 20 feet in front. This helps to maintain an objective view of this "imprint" experience. From this objectivity, the client can identify that specific belief being formed from that experience, as well as being protected from re-associating into that potentially traumatic event. We positively reframe any potential benefits that having that belief has provided over the years. This is what Dilts calls 'subjective reality.'

2. By encouraging the maintenance of an adult state firmly anchored in the present, the client is free to evaluate the resources which were needed by all the participants in that imprint experience. The necessary criterion is that the client has these resources as an adult in the present. As a "colleague" of the client, we collaborate to help develop potential internal resources that "significant others" in that experience could have used back then.

3. The client steps into those resources to fully experience them intensely and imagines that she can "transform" those identified resources into an 'energy' or 'light' which is transferred to those significant others in that early experience.

---

* Dilts, Robert. *Changing Belief Systems with NLP*. Capitola, CA: Meta Publications, 1990

157

4. She then replays the movie from the perspective of each of the major characters in this scene, as if each had fully integrated these resources. She associates into the younger self last. Now I invite her to determine the degree of difference in the quality of the belief, and to assess the effectiveness of making that change. Given a satisfactory assessment, the client is asked to bring those resources of the younger self through all the ensuing experiences all the way to the present, watching how her experiences and beliefs have been transformed.

5. If necessary, different resources can be accessed as appropriate or we can reinforce those already available until the client is satisfied. Then we formulate the language of a new empowering belief, and to integrate this belief in the present experience as well as rehearse it into the future.

References

Bandler, R., & Grinder, J. (1975) *The patterns of the hypnotic techniques of Milton H. Erickson Vol I*. Palo Alto, CA: Behavior & Science Books.

Bandler, R., & Grinder, J. (1985) *Using Your Mind—For A Change*. Moab, Utah: Real People Press.

Bass, E. & Davis. (1988) *The Courage to Heal: A Guide for Woman Survivors of child sexual abuse*. New York, NY: Harper & Row.

Bell-Gadsby, C. & Siegenberg, A. (1995) *Reclaiming Herstory: Ericksonian Solution-Focused therapy for sexual abuse*. New York: Bruner/Mazel.

Blume, E. Sue (1990) *Secret Survivors: Understanding incest and its aftereffects in women*. New York: Wiley & Sons.

Briere, J. (1989) *Therapy for Adults Molested as Children: Beyond Survival*. New York: Springer

Butler, S. (1985) *Conspiracy of Silence: The trauma of incest*. San Francisco: Volcano Press.

Caloff, D. (1993) "Facing the truth about false memory." *The Family Therapy Networker, 17* (5) 39–45.

Caloff, D. (1987) "Treating adult survivors of incest and child abuse." Workshop presented at the Family Therapy Network Symposium, Washington, D.C.

Carlson, E.B. , & Putnam, F. W. (1992) *Manual for the Dissociative Experience Scale.*

Carnes, P. (1983) *Out of the Shadows: Understanding sexual addiction*. Minnesota: Compcare Publications.

Chu, J. (1990) "Ten traps for therapist in the treatment of trauma survivors." *Dissociation 1*, 24–32.

Cole, E. (1982) "Sibling Incest: The myth of benign sibling incest." *Women and Therapy, 5* 79–89.

Combs, G., & Freeman, J. (1990) *Symbol, Story, and Ceremony: Using metaphor in individual and family therapy.* New York: W.W. Norton & Co.

Courtois, C.A. (1988) *Healing the Incest Wound: Adult survivors in therapy.* New York: W.W. Norton .

Crowder, A. (1995) *Opening the Door: A treatment model for therapy with male survivors of sexual abuse.* New York: Bruner/Mazel.

Cruz, F.G. & Essen, L. (1994) *Adult Survivors of Childhood Emotional, Physical & Sexual Abuse: Dynamics and treatment.* Northvale, New Jersey: Jason Aronson, Inc.

Davis, L. (1991) *Allies in Healing.* New York: HarperCollins.

deShazer, S. (1994) *Words were Originally Magic.* New York: W.W. Norton.

deShazer, S. (1988) *Clues: Investigating Solutions in Brief Therapy.* New York: W.W. Norton

deShazer, S. (1985) *Keys to Solution in Brief Therapy.* New York: W.W. Norton.

deShazer, S. (1984b) "Four useful interventions in brief family therapy." *Journal of Marital and Family Therapy, 10* (3), 297–304.

Dilts, R. (1990) *Changing Belief Systems with NLP.* Capitola, CA: Meta Publications.

Dolan, Y. (1991) *Resolving Sexual Abuse: Solution-focused therapy and Ericksonian hypnosis for adult survivors.* New York: W.W. Norton.

Durant, M. & White, C. (Eds) (1990) *Ideas for Therapy with Sexual Abuse.* South Australia: Dulwich Centre Publications.

Erickson, M.H., & Rossi, E.L. (1989) *The February Man: Evolving consciousness and identity in hypnotherapy.* New York: Bruner/Mazel.

Everstine, L. & Everstine, D. (1989) *Sexual Trauma in Children and Adolescents: Dynamics and treatment.* New York: Bruner/Mazel.

Finkelhor, D. (1986) *A Sourcebook on Child Sexual Abuse: New theory and research.* Beverly Hills: Sage Publications.

Friedrich, W.N., (1990) *Psychotherapy of Sexually Abused Children and their Families.* New York: W.W. Norton.

Forward, S. & Buck, C. (1978) *Betrayal of Innocence: Incest and its devastation.* Los Angeles: J.P. Tarcher.

Gil, E. (1996) *Systematic Treatment of Families Who Abuse.* San Francisco: Jossey-Bass.

Gil, E. (1988) *Treatment of Adult Survivors of Childhood Abuse.* Walnut Creek, CA: Launch Press.

Gil, E. (1983) *Outgrowing the Pain: A book for and about adults abused as children.* Walnut Creek: Launch Press.

Gilligan, S.G (1987) *Therapeutic Trances: The cooperation principle in Ericksonian hypnotherapy.* New York: Bruner/Mazel.

Haley, J. (1987) *Problem-Solving Therapy* (2nd ed.) San Francisco: Jossey-Bass.

Haley, J. (1973) *Uncommon Therapy.* New York: W.W. Norton.

Herman, J.L. (1992) *Trauma and Recovery.* New York: Basic Books.

Herman, J.L. (1981) *Father-Daughter Incest.* Cambridge, MA: Harvard University Press.

Hunter, M. (1990) *The Sexually Abused Male.* 2 vols. Lexington, MA: Lexington Books

Hunter, M. (1990) *Abused Boys: The neglected victims of sexual abuse.* New York: Fawcett Columbine.

Kempe, R. & Kempe, H. (1984) *The Common Secret.* New York: W.H. Freeman.

Kirschner, S, & Kirschener, D.L. & Rappaport, R.L. (1993) *Working with Adult Incest Survivors: The healing journey.* New York: Bruner/Mazel

Lawrence, L.R. (1993) "Backlash: A look at the abuse related amnesia and delayed memory controversy." *Moving Forward*. Vol 2, No. 4.

Lew, M. (1990) *Victims No Longer: Men recovering from incest and other sexual child abuse*. New York: Harper Collins.

Loftus, E.F. (1993) "The Reality of Repressed Memory." *American Psychologist 48* (95) 518–537.

Loredo, C. (1982) "Sibling Abuse." In S.M. Sgroi (ed) *Handbook of Clinicial Interventions in Child Sexual Abuse*. Lexington, MA: D.C. Heath.

MacDonald, K., Lambie, I., & Simonds, L. (1995) *Counselling for Sexual Abuse: A therapist guide*. Oxford: Oxford University Press.

Maltz, W. (1991) *The Sexual Healing Journey: A guide for survivors of sexual abuse*. New York: Harper Collins.

Maltz, W., & Holman, B. (1987) *Incest and Sexuality: A guide to understanding and healing*. Lexington, MA: Lexington Books.

McCann, L., & Pearlman, L. (1990a) "Vicarious traumatization: A framework for understanding the psychological effects of working with victims." *Journal of Traumatic Stress, 3*, 131–149.

McCann, L., & Pearlman, L. (1990b) *Psychological trauma in adult survivors: Theory, therapy and transformation*. New York: Bruner/Mazel.

Miller, A. (1984) *"Thou shall not be aware": Society's betrayal of the child*. New York: Farrar, Straus, Giroux.

Napier, N..J. (1993) *Getting through the day: Strategies for adults abused as children*. New York: W.W. Norton.

O'Hanlon, W. H. (1987) *Taproots*. New York: W.W. Norton

O'Hanlon, W. H., & Martin, M. (1992) *Solution-oriented Hypnosis: An Ericksonian approach*. New York: W.W. Norton.

O'Hanlon. W.H. (1996) "Personal Communication," Family Therapy Networker Symposium, Washington, D.C.

O'Hanlon, W. H., & Bertolino, B. (1998) *Even From a Broken Web: Solution-oriented therapy for sexual abuse and trauma.* New York: w.W. Norton.

Pearlman, L.A., & Saakvitne, K.W. (1995) *Trauma and the Therapist.* New York. W.W. Norton.

Piaget, J. (1970) *Structuralism.* New York: Basic Books.

Prendergast, W. (1993) *The Merry-go-round of Sexual Abuse: Identifying and treating survivors.* New York: Haworth Press.

Putnam, F.W. (1989) *Diagnosis and Treatment of Multiple Personality Disorder.* New York: Guilford Press.

Renshaw, D. (1982) *Incest: Understanding and treatment.* Boston: Little, Brown.

Roth, N. (1993) *Integrating the Shattered Self: Psychotherapy with adult incest survivors.* Northvale, New Jersey.

Russell, D. (1986) *The Secret Trauma: Incest in the lives of girls and women.* New York: Basic Books.

Salter, A. (1988) *Treating Child Sex Offenders and Victims: A practical guide.* Beverly Hills, CA: Sage Press.

Sanderson, C. (1995) *Counselling Adult Survivors of Child Sexual Abuse.* London: Jessica Kingsley Publishers.

Sanford, L. (1990) Strong at the Broken Places: Overcoming the trauma of childhood abuse. New York: Random House.

Sgroi, S., & Bunk, B. (1982) "A Clinical Approach to Adult Survivors of Child Sexual Abuse" in S. Sgroi (ED) *Vulnerable Populations: Evaluation and treatment of sexually abused children and adult survivors.* Vol. 1. Lexington, MA: D.C. Heath.

Simmonds, S.L.. (1994) *Bridging the Silence.* New York: W.W. Norton.

Steele, K. & Coltrain, J. (1990) "Abreactive Work with Sexually Abused Survivors: Concepts and techniques." In Hunter, M (ed) *The Sexually Abused Male.* 21–55. Lexington, MA: Lexington .

Terr, L. (1994) *Unchained Memories: True stories of traumatic memories, lost and found.* New York: Bruner/Mazel.

Trepper, T.S., & Barrett, M. J. (1989) *Systematic Treatment of Incest.* New York: Bruner/Mazel.

Van der Kolk, B.A., & van der Hart (1991) *The Intrusive Past: The flexibility of memory and the engraving of trauma.* American Imago, 48 (4) 425–454.

Yapko, M.D. (199) *Suggestions of Abuse: True and false memories of childhood sexual abuse.* New York: Simon & Schuster.

Yapko, M.D. (1993) Personal "Communications." Family Therapy Networker Symposium, Washington, D.C.

Zeig, J.K. (1980) *Ericksonian Approaches to Hypnosis and Psychotherapy.* New York: Bruner/Mazel.

Index

```
STUDY PACKAGE
CONTINUING EDUCATION
CREDIT INFORMATION
```

COLLABORATIVE HEALING
A "SHORTER" THERAPY APPROACH FOR SURVIVORS OF SEXUAL ABUSE

Thank you for choosing PESI Healthcare as your continuing education provider. Our goal is to provide you with current, accurate and practical information from the most experienced and knowledgeable speakers and authors.

Listed below are the continuing education credit(s) currently available for this self-study package. ***Please note, your state licensing board dictates whether self study is an acceptable form of continuing education. Please refer to your state rules and regulations.*

Counselors: PESI HealthCare, LLC is recognized by the National Board for Certified Counselors to offer continuing education for National Certified Counselors. Provider #: 5896. We adhere to NBCC Continuing Education Guidelines. These self-study materials qualify for 4.25 contact hours.

Psychologists: PESI is approved by the American Psychological Association to offer continuing education for psychologists. PESI maintains responsibility for the material. PESI is offering this self-study activity for 4.0 hours of continuing education credit.

Social Workers: PESI HealthCare, 1030, is approved as a provider for social work continuing education by the Association of Social Work Boards (ASWB), (540-829-6880) through the Approved Continuing Education (ACE) program. Licensed Social Workers should contact their individual state boards to determine self-study approval and to review continuing education requirements for licensure renewal. Social Workers will receive 4.25 continuing education clock hours for completing this self-study material.

Addiction Counselors: PESI HealthCare, LLC is a Provider approved by NAADAC Approved Education Provider Program. Provider #: 366. These self-study materials qualify for 5.0 contact hours.

Nurses: PESI HealthCare, LLC, Eau Claire is an approved provider of continuing nursing education by the Wisconsin Nurses Association Continuing Education Approval Program Committee, an accredited approver by the American Nurses Credentialing Center's Commission on Accreditation. This approval is accepted and/or recognized by all state nurses associations that adhere to the ANA criteria for accreditation. This learner directed educational activity qualifies for 5.1 contact hours. PESI Healthcare certification: CA #06538.

Procedures: 1. Read book.
                       2. Complete the post-test/evaluation form and mail it along with payment to the address on the form.

Your completed test/evaluation will be graded. If you receive a passing score (80% and above), you will be mailed a certificate of successful completion with earned continuing education credits. If you do not pass the post-test, you will be sent a letter indicating areas of deficiency, references to the appropriate sections of the manual for review and your post-test. The post-test must be resubmitted and receive a passing grade before credit can be awarded.

If you have any questions, please feel free to contact our customer service department at 1-800-843-7763.

PESI HealthCare, LLC
200 SPRING ST. STE B, P.O. BOX 1000
EAU CLAIRE, WI 54702-1000

Product Number: ZHS008795   **CE Release Date:** 03/10/04

**HealthCare**
P.O. Box 1000
Eau Claire, WI 54702
(800) 843-7763

Collaborative Healing
A "Shorter" Therapy Approach
for Survivors of Sexual Abuse
ZNT008795

This home study package includes CONTINUING
EDUCATION FOR ONE PERSON: complete & return
this original post/test evaluation form.

ADDITIONAL PERSONS interested in receiving credit
may photocopy this form, complete and return with a
payment of $25.00 per person CE fee. A certificate of
successful completion will be mailed to you.

For office use only
Rcvd. _____
Graded _____
Cert. mld. _____

C.E. Fee: **$25**   Credit card # _____

Exp. Date _____

Signature _____

V-Code* _____ (***MC/VISA/Discover:** last 3-digit # on signature
panel on back of card.) (***American Express:** 4-digit # above account # on face
of card.)

**Mail to: PESI HealthCare, PO Box 1000, Eau Claire, WI 54702, or
Fax to: PESI HealthCare (800) 675-5026 (fax all pages)**

Name (please print): _____ _____ _____
                              LAST   FIRST   M.I.

Address: _____

City: _____ State: _____ Zip: _____

Daytime Phone: _____

Signature: _____

• Date you completed the PESI HC Tape/Manual Independent Package: _____

• Actual time (# of hours) taken to complete this offering: _____ hours

PROGRAM OBJECTIVES

How well did we do in achieving our objectives?

	Excellent				**Poor**
Identify strategies and techniques to define realistic interventions.	5	4	3	2	1
Explain the major elements of the recovery process for all survivors.	5	4	3	2	1
Explain the incidences of inaccurate diagnosis, mislabeling, and other assessment errors with survivors.	5	4	3	2	1
Identify approaches to help clients reduce abreactions, dissociative episodes.	5	4	3	2	1
Explain how to assist clients in managing their flashbacks.	5	4	3	2	1
Conduct techniques that assist your client in achieving a sense of safety and comfort during and after the therapeutic experience.	5	4	3	2	1
Identify issues of counter-transference.	5	4	3	2	1
Explain your own risks for secondary victimization.	5	4	3	2	1

POST-TEST QUESTIONS

1. Survivors of incest must relieve/reexperience (catharsis) the trauma in order to resolve it.

   True or **False**

POST-TEST QUESTIONS (CONTINUED)

2. A basis assumption of briefer therapy is "Clients are not able to effectively determine their treatment course without the therapist's expertise."

   True or **False**

3. All current symptoms or problems that a client brings to treatment were caused by the abuse.

   True or **False**

4. Anchoring is a process by which sensory elements become associated with certain feelings, behaviors or events.

   True or **False**

5. A Solution Focus is a way to a_____, v_____, v_____ a client's perception and experiences.

6. Three counter transference issues confronting clinicians are:

   a.

   b.

   c.

7. In the world of "Possibility", which of the following do not apply?
   a. Client and therapist both are experts.
   b. The treatment must be long term to acquire desired results.
   c. The therapist must assist the client in "putting the past to rest" before treatment can be completed.
   d. To better understand your client, they must tell you the whole story.
   e. Validate and support each part of the client's experiences & self.

For additional forms and information on other PESI products, contact:
Customer Service; PESI HEALTHCARE; P.O. Box 1000; Eau Claire, WI 54702
(Toll Free, 7 a.m.-5 p.m. central time, 800-843-7763).
www.pesihealthcare.com

Thank you for your comments.
We strive for excellence and we value your opinion.

03/04

Professional Resources Available from PESI HealthCare

Resources for Mental Health Professionals

Addiction, Progression & Recovery, by Dale Kesten, LCSW, LADC

Assessing and Treating Trauma and PTSD, by Linda Schupp, Ph.D

Borderline Personality Disorder—Struggling, Understanding, Succeeding, by Colleen E. Warner, Psy.D

Case Management Handbook for Clinicians, by Rand L. Kannenberg, MA

Clinicians Update on the Treatment and Management of Anxiety Disorders, by Deborah Antai-Otong, MS, RN, CNS, NP, CS, FAAN

Collaborative Healing: A Shorter Therapy Approach for Survivors of Sexual Abuse, by Mark Hirschfeld, LCSW-C, BCD & Jill B. Cody, MA

Delirium–The Mistaken Confusion, by Debra Cason-McNeeley, MSN, RNCS

Depression and Other Mood Disorders, by Deborah Antai-Otong, MS, RN, CNS, NP, CS, FAAN

Effective Strategies for Helping Couples and Families, by John S. Carpenter

Grief: Normal, Complicated, Traumatic, by Linda Schupp, Ph.D

Psychiatric Emergencies, by Deborah Antai-Otong, MS, RN, CNS, NP, CS, FAAN

Sociotherapy for Sociopaths: Resocial Group, by Rand L. Kannenberg, MA

Resources for Nurses & Other Healthcare Professionals

Heart and Lung Sounds Reference Library (Audio CD), by Diane Wrigley, PA-C

Infection Control and Emerging Infectious Diseases, by William Barry Inman

Legal and Ethical Standards for Nurses, by Sheryl Feutz-Harter

Managing Urinary Incontinence (Audio CD), by Carol Ann White, RN, MS, ANPC, GNPC

Mechanisms and Treatment of Disease: Pathophysiology—A Plain English Approach, by Mikel A. Rothenberg, MD

Oral Medication and Insulin Therapies: A Practical Guide for Reaching Diabetes Target Goals, by Charlene Freeman

Subclinical Signs of Impending Doom (Audio CD), by Carol Whiteside, RN, PhD(c)

Understanding X-Rays–A Plain English Approach, by Mikel A. Rothenberg

To order these or other PESI HealthCare products or to receive information about our national seminars, please call 800-843-7763

www.pesihealthcare.com